Managerial Leadership in the Post-industrial Society

PHILIP SADLER

Gower

Published by
Gower Publishing Company Limited,
Gower House,
Croft Road,
Aldershot
Hants GU11 3HR,
England

Reprinted 1989

British Library Cataloguing in Publication Data

Sadler, Philip
  Managerial leadership in the post-
  industrial society.
  1. Service industries. Management.
  Leadership
  I. Title
  338.4

  ISBN 0-566-02611-2

Typeset by Inforum Ltd, Portsmouth

Printed and bound in Great Britain at
The Camelot Press Ltd, Southampton

Contents

The first rule of survival is clear: nothing is more dangerous than yesterday's success.

Alvin Toffler (1985)

Preface

This book has been written for practising managers and particularly for those facing rapid and radical change in markets, technologies or the competitive environment. It has two purposes which are mutually reinforcing. First, it aims to help managers who are not themselves economists and social scientists to understand the true nature and implications of the massive changes that are currently transforming the business environment, and so lead them towards a coherent vision of the socio-economic framework which organizations will face in the near future. Secondly, it examines the effects of the transformation of society on the nature of the manager's job and, hence, his training and development needs.

The vision of the future business environment which is unveiled in the first half of the book has been inspired by the insight and analysis of writers such as Peter Drucker (1969), Daniel Bell (1973) and Alvin Toffler (1980). Although it is in many ways unsatisfactory, I have adopted Bell's descriptive phrase 'the post-industrial society' as a shorthand means of referring to that future state.

If the vision is open to criticism it is not perhaps vulnerable so much to the obvious one – that it is a false vision and that the post-industrial society will never come. A more valid objection is that it is no longer a statement about the future, but rather one about the present, or even the past. The features of a post-industrial society are already well established in North America and Western Europe – service industries account for the lion's share of gross domestic product and employment, knowledge and information have become the key resources, and knowledge-intensive institutions the chief source of wealth creation. Information technology has superseded energy and materials technology as the principal factor in productivity growth. The nature of work has been transformed and with it the nature of family life.

Yet in a very important sense the post-industrial society still lies in the future. This is because to a large extent cultural change lags behind economic and technological change. Societies which are objectively 'post-industrial' and which have experienced radical 'de-industrialization' are subjectively still 'industrial' societies, in the sense that the values and attitudes, lifestyles, systems of organization and social structures which dominate are those which grew out of the industrial era. Not until industrial and political leaders, consumers, workers, employers – indeed all sections of the community – recognize the true nature of the transformation and start acting accordingly will the post-industrial society come into its own.

This book is designed as a very modest contribution to the hastening of this process. If it is read by managers who, having read it, feel that they have a better insight into what is happening in the world around them, and above all if, in consequence, they start taking decisions based on an altered frame of reference, then it will have accomplished its purpose.

I should like to acknowledge the source of the insight which started the whole process – Peter Drucker; the help I have received from my colleagues, particularly Andrew Ettinger and Barbara Dewell; and the encouragement I have had from my family to finish the project, once started.

Philip Sadler

Part One
The Post-Industrial Society

1 The coming of the post-industrial society

At the approach of the final decade of the 20th century, western industrial society is experiencing a transformation as radical and far reaching in its effects as the industrial revolution. Indeed, the term 'a second industrial revolution' has often been used to describe it.

The outcome of this transformation will be a new kind of society, as different from the industrial society we have known during our lifetimes as the industrial society itself was different from the agricultural society which preceded it. This new society is already taking shape; its salient features are capable of being described. Daniel Bell (1973) has called it the 'post-industrial society'. Alvin Toffler (1980) calls it the society of the 'third wave'.

The purpose of this book is to explore the nature of this new society and to examine its implications for organizations and the people whose task it is to make them work – the managers.

The emergence of the post-industrial society

The emergence of the post-industrial society can best be understood by placing it in its historical context and showing how, in the development of human society, technological progress, economic development and social change have been closely interconnected. Figure 1.1 shows, in greatly simplified form, the way in which human society has developed since its origins millions of years ago. The analysis

Stage of development	Major technological innovation	Principal economic activity	Social systems	Date of origin
Pre-agrarian	—	Hunting/ gathering	Simple tribal nomadic	Origin of mankind (2 to 4 million years)
Agrarian	Metal working	Farming	Rural settlements	c. 7000 BC
Industrial	Steam power	Manu-facturing	Industrial cities	c. AD 1800
Post-industrial	Computer	Services	Suburban communi-ties	AD 1965

Figure 1.1   A theory of social development: Daniel Bell's concept of the 'post-industrial society'

follows Bell and Toffler in distinguishing three main phases in the development process up to the present time – the pre-agrarian, the agrarian and the industrial. (This is not to deny that there was considerable societal change and development within the agrarian and industrialized periods, which can in turn be sub-divided into phases.)

The pre-agrarian stage is characterized by a virtual absence of technology. Man gradually acquires the ability to fashion tools and weapons from stone and over long periods of time his skill in this process clearly improves. He also discovers uses for fire. Beyond this, however, there is no accumulation of practical knowledge of use to man in achieving mastery over his material environment.

In the absence of means to enable man to exercise control over nature he is wholly dependent upon it. His economic activity is confined to hunting, fishing and gathering, or foraging. This method of obtaining a living in turn determines the characteristics of pre-agrarian society. First, it is nearly always nomadic, the people following the migration of herds seeking fresh grazing. Nomadic societies are incapable of developing an elaborate material technology. They are limited by what they can carry around with them, confined to what can be used by a society continuously on the move.

Secondly, they are simple societies in terms of social structure. There is, for example, only a rudimentary division of labour – the male role of hunter/warrior and the female role of food gatherer and child rearer. There is no specialized knowledge or special skills to form the basis of an occupational structure and as everyone is constantly involved in the struggle for survival, time and energy cannot be spared for other activities.

Thirdly, they are largely closed societies, tribal in nature, based on kinship ties, inbred. Such societies existed for over one million years, probably much longer, before there was any significant change in the human condition. Change and development did, of course, take place, albeit painfully slowly. Gradually man learned to make sharper and smoother stone implements – even stone sickles, and in many parts of the world he achieved a degree of control over the wandering herds which provided the basis of his sustenance and adopted a pastoral way of life. But radical change did not take place until about twelve thousand years ago, in approximately 10 000 BC.

The agrarian revolution

This radical change was, of course, the agrarian revolution – in Toffler's terms, the 'first wave'. Archaeological evidence tells us that it began in a number of places in the Middle East. Theories as to how and why it began are various. Bronowski (1973) argues that it resulted from a mutation of wheat grass following the Ice Age. This mutation had three characteristics – the large grain was a powerful source of nourishment, it was fertile (unlike most mutations) and hence could be used for propagation, and the heaviness of the grain meant it was not carried and sown by the wind – man had to take a hand. Man learned to sow seed and to harvest crops and in the process of learning this he stopped moving about and settled in one place. Once settled on the land he began to produce a surplus, which meant above all that he could divert some of his time and energy away from food production and on to other activities – in particular, inventing and making things. In a relatively short space of time (compared with the span of pre-history) he had discovered bronze and iron, had invented the wheel, the pulley and the lever, and had learned to harness animals to the yoke and to use them for his own transportation.

Out of a settled agriculture grew civilization. Gradually a rich and diverse division of labour developed reflecting the growing specialization of the population in such activities as spinning and weaving cloth, building farm dwellings, beating plough-shares, providing defence against attack, making and enforcing laws, trading, banking, and serving God. Small communities combined for defence and trade and the City State, followed by the Nation State came into existence. This civilization remained, however, firmly based on agriculture – the great bulk of the population worked on the land. National prosperity depended almost entirely on the quality and quantity of the harvest and such manufacturing and service activities as existed were largely supportive of agriculture. Above all the source of power was ownership of land, coupled with ownership or control of agricultural labour – slaves or serfs.

During the agrarian period, technological progress was infinitely more rapid than during the pre-agrarian age. In the field of energy, man learned how to harness the power in wind and water. In the field of materials technology he rapidly developed his skills in making and working metals. He learned to combine new sources of energy and new metal-working skills so as to produce quite complex machinery for grinding his corn. He learned how to build sailing ships and how to navigate the great oceans, ultimately encircling the globe. His ability to learn and to disseminate knowledge leapt ahead with the invention of printing. And all the time he was learning how to grow more food per acre without destroying the soil's fertility, how to feed livestock and protect it from disease, and how to extend the range of foodstuffs available to him by bringing new crops from distant shores into cultivation.

The development of practical knowledge advanced particularly rapidly during the 18th century and nowhere more so than in England. By this time England had become a stable, prosperous agrarian society – one in which an enlightened, rational, landed aristocracy was applying scientific knowledge to food production, encouraging and patronizing such innovators as Coke of Holkham and 'Turnip' Townshend. To have been alive at that time, however, would have involved an inevitable belief in the settled order of things – a way of life centred around the village and farming, one characterized by progress, certainly, but not one to be shattered by change of cataclysmic dimensions. Yet within one hundred years the face of England and much of Europe had been altered beyond recognition. By the time of the Great Exhibition of 1851 the Industrial Revolution had largely taken place, England had become an industrial rather than an agrarian society, and life would never be the same again. Toffler's 'second wave' of change was in full flood.

The Industrial Revolution

Much more is known about the Industrial Revolution than the agrarian revolution. There is certainly no doubt about *where* the Industrial Revolution began – it was in Britain. Nor is there any doubt as to *when* – it began in the second half of the 18th century and gathered pace rapidly in the first half of the 19th century. When it comes to *how* and *why*, however, the answers are less certain and much more complex. Many different factors came together at the same time. Growth in the number of surplus agricultural workers led to the invention of the factory system, as woollen merchants shifted from reliance on cottage industry to centralized mass production. The invention of steam power not only resulted in much faster and more reliable machinery being installed in the new factories, it made possible the mechanization of transport and farming. Invention followed invention. The bringing together in one locality of large numbers of workers to operate the new machines in turn created large markets to be served with goods and services. An increasingly wealthy nation expanded its empire and the empire in turn provided both raw materials for its industries and markets for its products. And given the protection from invasion afforded by the North Sea and the English Channel, all this burgeoning economic activity was able to continue without interruption or distraction.

The agrarian era involved the development and application of many technologies but if one has to be singled out as most important it is metal working. Without tools and implements of iron it would have been impossible to clear much of the land of forest and it would not have been possible to bring the heavier soil of Northern Europe into cultivation. Agriculture would have been confined largely to the Mediterranean and to the banks of the rivers. Similarly, if one has to single out the core technology of the industrial era there is no doubt that it is the exploitation of energy – initially from coal via steam, then via gas and electricity, later from oil, used either as an energy source for electricity generation or more directly in the internal combustion engine, and most recently from nuclear power.

In economic terms, clearly the dominant activity of the industrial era is manufacturing. With the growth in importance of manufacturing industry a new source of power arises in society to vie for supremacy with ownership of the land, namely ownership and control of capital – the capitalist emerging as a new élite alongside and to some extent superseding the landed gentry.

Toffler (1980) provides a brilliant analysis of the spirit of industrialism which he sees as based on six principles as follows:

1 *Standardization* – Not only of products but of procedures and working methods, school curricula, housing, weights and measures, currency, prices, etc.
2 *Specialization* – The industrial society involves a sharp intensification of the division of labour.
3 *Synchronization* – Everything done on time and one activity timed to fit in with another.
4 *Concentration* – of the population in cities, of work in factories, of capital in the giant corporation.
5 *Maximization* – Big is beautiful, the economies of scale, the worship of growth.
6 *Centralization* – Central control based on centralized information and centralized power.

Rapid technological change, radical change in the nature of economic activity and the development of a new set of beliefs about how things should be ordered combined to bring about a social revolution. The salient features of this revolution in the 19th century were the growth of the towns, the development of mass education, the spread of mass democracy, the growth of trade unions and the emergence of socialism as a potential source of political power.

In the 20th century the social revolution has advanced further with the development of social welfare, the growth of further and higher education, women's rights, consumer power and the arrival of socialism as a political force.

By the 1950s the industrial society had reached its zenith in the United States and in Western Europe. Manufacturing industry was unchallenged as the source of wealth and prosperity (and full employment) in countries which were the envy of the rest of the world. It was as difficult to imagine a different future in the 1950s as it had been back in the 1750s. Yet the industrialized world was standing on the threshold of even more radical and rapid change than the agrarian society two hundred years earlier.

The second industrial revolution
Whereas the agrarian revolution is too distant to be able to describe and understand it, the problem with the post-industrial revolution (Toffler's 'third wave') is that it is too close. What *is* clear is that the impact is being felt of a new wave of major technological change just as significant as the discovery of metal working or the invention of the steam engine. The new technology is, of course, information technology. This information revolution is still in the early stages but it will eventually change our lives more radically and more rapidly than iron tools and weapons changed the lives of our ancestors or the steam engine the lives of our forebears. It is also clear that once again radical change is taking place in the nature of our economic activity. Each year fewer people in Western Europe or North America are employed in traditional manufacturing industry, while employment has been growing in many service industries.

Another observable trend is the growing importance of ownership and control of *knowledge* and *information* as a source of power in society – the technocrat, standing along-side the capitalist and the aristocrat. Related to this is the emergence of the 'knowledge-intensive' organization along-side the 'capital-intensive' and 'labour-intensive' organizations of the past.

There are consequential shifts in population density as the numbers living in the largest industrial conurbations decline, and in the prosperity of regions as the centre of economic gravity shifts from places like Pittsburgh to 'silicon valley', or the 'sunshine belt', and from the West Midlands of Britain to the Thames Valley.

New beliefs about the way things should be ordered are taking shape, challenging the creed of industrialism. The precepts of the post-industrial society are as yet not precisely formulated, but they include a strong emphasis on the virtues of decentralization, the belief that small is beautiful, that goods and services should be as individualized as possible, and that the quality of life is more important than material growth.

In the chapters which follow, the nature of the post-industrial revolution will be explored in three dimensions – the social, the economic and the technological.

An invisible line divides all managers today. It cuts across rank and function to separate those who see today's economic and technological changes as incremental, bit-by-bit extensions of the Industrial Revolution from those who regard today's massive changes as truly radical. There are 'incrementalist executives' and 'radical executives'.

Alvin Toffler (1985)

2　The new social order

Social change can mean a number of things, each reflecting a different aspect of the complex process which occurs as human society evolves.

Attitudes and values

First, there are changes in what people believe, the opinions and attitudes they hold, the expectations they have. Sociologists would speak of changes in systems of values and ethics or of changes in the mores of society. Changes of this kind which affect behaviour in organizations, and hence the role of the manager, include beliefs about the place of work in one's life and what should be expected from it; attitudes towards authority and the sources of its legitimacy; opinions concerning the rights and obligations of employers, employees and racial or religious minority groups; and expectations about such things as security and stability of employment, personal and career development and involvement of the employee in decision making.

Clearly there have been changes under all these headings in recent years and equally obviously these will continue into the future. Mostly, they have had the effect of making the manager's job more challenging, more demanding of the ability to adapt and change, and hence more difficult.

Social institutions

Change of a second kind can be seen in the institutions which make up a human society – changes in their rates of growth or decline, in the social functions they fulfil and in their own internal structure. These institutions include the family, the community, the work organization, educational institutions, trade unions, religious institutions, pressure groups, institutions in the field of leisure and indeed all organized, enduring forms of human interaction.

Changes under this heading in the recent past have been both rapid and profound. Among them the revolution in the role and structure of the family has been of most fundamental importance in terms of reflecting the nature of social change in the second half of the 20th century and its interdependence with economic growth and development on the one hand and technological change on the other.

Figure 2.1 depicts in the most general and simplistic way the structure of the family in the agrarian society – the extended family. In many societies, power in such families resides in the oldest surviving male, so long as he retains his physical and mental powers. This is not only because of his social role as head of a group which is a *work* organization as well a *domestic* unit, or because he normally holds the title to any property (particularly land) held by the family, but because in a society in which the pace of economic and technological change is slow, to be old is to be the repository of accumulated knowledge and, therefore, to wield the power that superior knowledge confers. By the time he reached his declining years the farm worker of previous generations had 'seen it all' – flood and drought, famine and pestilence, war and epidemic. He had survived and knew how to survive. Small wonder, therefore, that when a new crisis arose the young turned to the old for help and to learn how to cope, particularly when the tools and techniques available had not changed. How different from society today when, given the rapid change in technology, the old learn from the young. Today's senior managers learn how to use their microcomputer from rising young executives in the training department, just as they learn how to use their home video-recorder by being instructed by their children.

In many societies the inheritance of the family property and

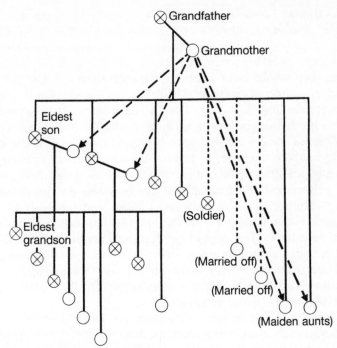

Values: Age, Tradition, Custom
       Maleness, Physical abilities
       Family, Independence
       Religion especially reference Fertility, Harvest
       Land, Property
       Sexual morality

Key
⊗ male
O female

Figure 2.1 Family structure – agrarian society

hence of the associated power and status was via the first born
male child. This gave him, of course, special importance,
including the choice of his bride (that he should *not* marry
would have been unthinkable). Naturally, his own taste in
women would not have been allowed to influence such an
important decision. The marriage would have been arranged
through the families concerned and the bride would have
been chosen on other criteria than her sexual attractiveness –
on the size and nature of her dowry, perhaps – and she would
have been selected much as farm livestock is chosen on the

basis that she was built for breeding rather than speed.

The younger brothers were treated differently. The wealthier the family, or (frequently much the same thing) the greater its need for future labour supply, the more likely that they, too, would have been encouraged to marry and have children while remaining within the extended family. In poorer families, however, the choice was between staying with the family but remaining a bachelor (which in the traditional society often meant celibacy) or leaving home to find fortune elsewhere. In Ireland where such poor but large families abounded the choice was between emigration and the priesthood. In England it lay between accepting the King's shilling and the colonies. (Those that stayed behind frequently developed close affectionate relationships with the farm livestock. The sexual perversion known as bestiality which today is looked upon with such strong aversion was, two hundred years ago, a much less serious matter than adultery which, with its power to break up families, offered a much stronger threat to society.)

Those who left home in England and Ireland in the late 18th and early 19th centuries helped create the labour supply for the Industrial Revolution. In the last two decades of the 18th century, for example, the Duke of Bridgewater and his engineer Brindley recruited young men from Ireland to dig the new canals which did so much to reduce transportation costs and open up trade. The Duke, himself known as the Father of Inland Navigation, called his men 'navigators' which, shortened to 'navvy' has remained the term descriptive of the construction site labourer ever since. (In an unintentional flash of humour an American textbook stated that most of the canals and railway cuttings of Europe and North America were originally created by the Irish *navy!*)

To grow up in such a family in such an age, characterized by the constant struggle against nature, with little change in the available technology during any one person's lifetime, meant acquiring certain values and beliefs from childhood and regarding them for the rest of one's life as self-evident truths. These included:

- A deep respect for the old people in society.
- A related respect for existing customs, traditions and age-old rituals.

- A belief in the superiority of the male whose physical strength and stamina was the family's main shield against adversity. (Daughters had their uses about the house, but it was important for them to be marriageable so that they could be got off one's hands soon after puberty.)
- A strong sense of family, strongly emphasized by rituals on occasions such as births, marriages and deaths which bound the family ties tighter.
- A very strong emphasis on the sanctity of property, particularly land and livestock. Hanging for sheep stealing was the practice not all that many years ago and when deportation to Australia superseded it in England many felt that the floodgates to crime and violence had been opened.
- A deep sense of religion, emphasized particularly at the time of the planting of seed and even more so at harvest time.
- A strictly enforced sexual morality in which adultery was the chief crime (coveting thy neighbour's wife) followed by premarital sex on the part of females. (For males the agrarian metaphor of sowing wild oats conjures up the full implication of what active young males were expected, even encouraged, to do – but where were the corresponding females to come from?)

The family in early industrial society was, and still is in many newly-industrializing countries, different in both function and structure. Functionally, it was no longer simultaneously both the work organization and the domestic unit. The focus of work now lay outside the family, in the factory or workshop. The function of socializing the young was now being shared by early forms of education in the schools.

In structure, the most important shift was that the head of the household was no longer the oldest male (grandfather or great grandfather) who, being too old to work regularly at a wage-earning job outside the home, was now a dependant living with one of his sons or married daughters, each of whom was now the head of, or the wife of the head of, a separate household. In these new industrial workers' families (see Figure 2.2) the male increasingly took the role of 'breadwinner' and went out to work, while it became increasingly the practice for the woman, during her child bearing

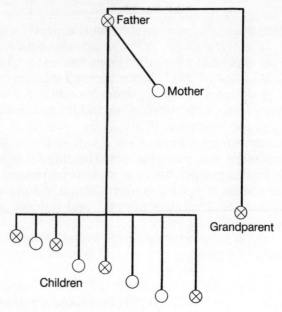

Values: Authority, Discipline, Subservience
        Maleness, Physical abilities
        Competitiveness, Aggression, Toughness
        Thrift
        Ambition
        Security

Key
⊗ male
O female

Figure 2.2   Family structure – industrial society (early phase)

years, to stay at home and do the work which kept the household going – cooking, cleaning, shopping, laundering, etc. This made for a division of labour between male and female sharper than in the agrarian family which, accompanied as it was by physical separation for most of the working hours, led on to the development of the male/female subcultures of the industrial society, exemplified by pigeon racing clubs on the one hand and women's magazines on the other.

When working-class married women of child-bearing age did go outside the home to work it was usually for very low wages (termed pin money) and part time – usually as a domestic help for a wealthier family. Such work did nothing for the status of women – rather the reverse.

Unmarried women of limited education were employed variously as factory workers (in the clothing and textile industries particularly), living-in domestics and shop assistants. The somewhat better educated worked as typists and secretaries (and were often categorized as white-collar workers, paid monthly and accorded a higher status in the same organization as their fathers who, having struggled to the powerful position of general foreman would still be classed as blue-collar employees, paid weekly, enjoying less security of employment and often confined to a different and altogether less attractive and hygienic canteen for their lunch). At this time, opportunities for women at yet higher levels of status were very limited. They occurred mainly in the rapidly growing professional ranks of teachers and civil servants – women in management positions in industry remained unthinkable.

In the working and lower-middle class families of this period, power and authority naturally accrued to the one on whose willingness and ability to work the family fortunes depended, namely the father. This was the age of the authoritarian father and husband, dispensing discipline somewhat arbitrarily in the home, in some cases subjecting his wife and children to violence, but in turn powerless at work with the possibility of being dismissed by his foreman ever present. Children were frequently (and with good cause) frightened of their fathers and encouraged to be so by exhausted mothers capable of keeping discipline only through the injunction 'just you wait till your father gets home!'

In this environment children therefore grew up with 'a proper respect for authority' – learned frequently at the end of their father's belt. They made, on the whole, good dutiful employees in their turn, transferring their respectful fear of father on to a respectful awe of the bowler-hatted foreman. They saw clearly, too, that it was a man's world. Men possessed the jobs which held families together, and in most working-class areas they did so by virtue of distinct male characteristics of physical strength, capacity for endurance, and the robust health required to survive a lifetime's work in a steel mill or metal-working factory. Children took pride in their fathers and claimed 'my dad can knock your dad's block off!' Children also learned not to waste food (one of the most serious crimes was to leave food on one's plate) or anything else – string, brown paper, cardboard boxes – for which a use could be found. They learned that the 'proper way of life' was to leave school as soon as the law allowed, to get a job (to be unemployed was to suffer a serious social stigma as well as real economic hardship), to get married, have children, be faithful, stay married, keep on working till retirement (preferably for the same employer) and to put something into insurance once a month towards the cost of a decent burial.

They also began to learn things which in the end would conspire, along with technological and economic change to alter the whole system – how to combine and develop huge and powerful unions to counterbalance the power of employers and (just as significant) how to influence their own living standards and the life chances of a reduced number of offspring by practising birth control.

But, finally, it was the combination of economic growth and technological progress that broke down this way of life. With the creation of the Welfare State in the post-war world, accompanied by full employment and sustained economic growth, living standards rose out of all recognition. Smaller families were increasingly better housed. Old people, living longer healthier lives in retirement and supported by State pensions, stayed in their own subsidized rented homes and did not move in with their sons or daughters. Wives and mothers responded to industry's apparently insatiable appetite for labour by going out to work, and increasingly for wages approximating to those of men. Teenagers on leaving school were quickly employed, and soon earning adult wages which caused problems in relation to discipline in the home. Vacuum cleaners, washing machines, and a host of other items of domestic technology gradually saturated homes and changed the nature of housework, while the growth of the supermarket changed the nature of shopping. The new 'nuclear' families created in this period – father, mother and two children – had a car, took their annual holiday in Spain and watched television.

In this socio-economic setting the power of the male breadwinner declined as that of the working mother and the working teenager grew. It was variously called the 'Affluent Society' or the 'Permissive Society'.

The shape of the nuclear family of the affluent society is

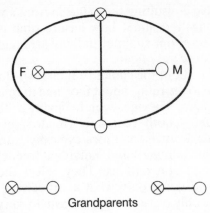

Grandparents

Values: Consultation
      Freedom
      Choice
      Unisex

Key
⊗ male
O female

Figure 2.3 Family structure – industrial society (mature phase)

shown in Figure 2.3. It is from such a background that today's
employees – workers and managers alike – increasingly come.
Its structure is no longer hierarchical or authoritarian. There
is no 'boss' as in the past; rather it is like a firm with joint
managing directors, each with his/her own sphere of responsibility, but coming together to share decisions affecting the
enterprise as a whole. Just so with the modern parents. The
father still tends to assume the greater responsibility for the
family's financial affairs and for the maintenance and repair
of the house and items such as the car, but he also shares the
shopping, the housework and above all care of the young
children, yet defers on all such matters to his wife seeing these
as lying within her sphere of expertise.

The children in Figure 2.3 (two is the norm) are not
arranged hierarchically dependent to the parents but, deliberately, in an encircling or smothering relationship. The needs
of the children dominate their parents' lives – not only needs
for education and health, but also less fundamental and
important needs and desires. As a result, decisions in such

houses involve consulting the children from a very early age. They are consulted about how leisure time is to be spent, particularly so about summer holiday arrangements (a five-year old was recently heard to exclaim wearily 'Oh no! not Ibiza again!'), about the choice of their own clothes; they are even allowed to 'be fussy' about food and to reject some while accepting others. They grow up believing in the freedom of the individual – both economic freedom in the sense of freedom from want (sometimes cynically translated as 'the world owes me a living') and individual freedom from rules, restrictions and conventions. They reject the old and the traditional and value only what is modern. They see their grandparents only occasionally, are usually very fond of them but not influenced by them. They frequently develop quite hostile attitudes to the institutions involved in wealth creation – a hostility which can sometimes be transferred to their own parents if they have been materially successful. They are attracted by contrast to campaigns to change the existing order, particularly those which emphasize greater concern for people or for the natural environment.

This family unit is, of course, much less stable and cohesive than previous ones. The older generation will normally live separate lives – not only in their own flats or seaside bunga-lows but often at some distance from their children's families so that 'visiting grandad and grandma' becomes an excursion to be planned. It is now relatively easy for the younger generation to leave home at an early age – in some cases to go on to further or higher education in other towns or to follow careers which pay well enough for teenagers to live in shared accommodation away from home. Finally, it is unstable in the sense that divorce is easier, not just legally, but for the more important reason that there is enough money available, whether it comes from private sector earnings or state benefits, to support two households where there was one before.

All this means that it is not so common nowadays to find the nuclear family household in the sense of a *married* couple with two children living at home together. Some of the variants include:

1   Two people, not married, living together with no chil-dren.

2 Two people, married or not married, living together but with children of both current and previous marriages or cohabitations.
3 Single parents living with children of a marriage broken by death, divorce or desertion. (The parent is usually, but not always, female.)
4 'Traditional' households in which there may be more than two children and in addition one or more living-in grandparent.
5 Single persons living alone, not yet having reached retiring age.
6 Single persons of the same sex sharing accommodation (with or without sharing a sexual relationship).
7 Single persons (usually students or young workers) of different sexes sharing the same accommodation but without sexual involvement with each other.
8 Retired people living alone – either married couples or a widow (more common) or widower (less common).
9 Some kind of commune. (This is still quite rare.)

The children of the emerging post-industrial society will, therefore, tend to come from a bewildering variety of social backgrounds. But they will tend to share at least some values and expectations. They will tend to put individuals (including themselves) before organizations; they will not take orders or subject themselves to discipline or bureaucratic rules so easily as their parents. They will expect to be consulted about issues and will be discriminating and discerning consumers. The separation of male and female roles will be less distinct.

Social structure

Another way of tracking social change is to look at changes in the social structure, that is to say the way a society is made up of people with various characteristics such as belonging to different age groups, different social classes, different ethnic groups, or different occupational groupings. These tend by their nature to be long-term trends arising in part from such demographic factors as changes in birth rates or life expectancy and partly from economic and technological changes as in the case of changes in occupational structure. As we move towards the post-industrial society two related structural changes, both of which are already well under way, will in the end fundamentally change the nature of society and the way in which we manage its various organizations.

First, the changes in occupational structure, leading to the disappearance of so much traditional 'blue-collar' manual work in such industries as steel, shipbuilding, engineering, and vehicles, with parallel growth in white-collar jobs, mainly in the service industries such as banking, insurance, health, education and the social services.

Secondly, and as a consequence, and hence following later in time, is the contraction (to be followed by the eventual disappearance) of the traditional working class. Just as the transition from the agrarian to the industrial society saw the eventual demise of the traditional forelock-tugging agricultural labourer in his tied cottage, only one step removed from serfdom, so the transition from an industrial to a post-industrial society will see the demise of the cloth-capped industrial worker and with him the customs, traditions and beliefs shared in common by his kind. These range from something simple like having dinner at midday instead of in the evening to the extremely complex and subtle rituals of a working-class wedding.

Add to these changes a society with an ageing population and one in which ethnic minority groups are growing in numbers faster than the indigenous population and the result is structural change on a grand scale.

Lifestyles

The three previously discussed forms of social change, that is changes in values, changes in social institutions and changes in the social structure, are all ultimately reflected in what Americans would call changes in *lifestyle* but which the British might prefer to talk of as a changed way of life. Over the past 25 years or so the 'changed way of life' has included such varied elements as more indulgence in pre or extra marital sex, holidays abroad, one-stop shopping, the growth of home entertainment (along with the disappearance of cinema queues), drug taking, convenience foods, the growth of continuing education, jogging and dieting. As the post-industrial society develops, these ways of life will in turn change, modify or disappear. To be able to predict the new ones is the creative marketing person's dream. Certainly, however, some of the elements are already visible. They include a much wider acceptance of the concept of life-long learning, more home use of computers and other forms of advanced information technology and the emergence of a whole new set of 'senior citizens' – retired but active and healthy people with considerable purchasing power who will constitute one of the most important segments of the leisure market.

Implications for the business enterprise

This alteration in lifestyles will call for related changes on the part of the business enterprise. In particular:

- New personnel policies and management styles adapted to the expectations and patterns of motivation of a new type of workforce.
- Rapid responses to changing needs of consumers as they become more sophisticated and discriminating as well as more affluent.
- New concepts of social responsibility in a social environment in which quality of life considerations increasingly become more important than the continued creation of material wealth.

Summary

The new social order associated with the coming of the post-industrial society involves social change of four main kinds:

1 Changes in attitudes, values and beliefs – including attitudes to work and authority and the balance between exploitation and conservation of the earth's resources.
2 Changes in social institutions – most importantly the family. Childhood experiences of young employees entering work in the closing years of this century will lead them to expect and demand involvement in decision making.
3 Changes in social structure – particularly the disappear-

ance of many traditional occupational groupings and with them the decline of a traditional working-class.

4   Changes in lifestyle.

Taken together, these changes constitute a new social environment for business, calling for a response in areas such as personnel policy, marketing strategy and a whole range of issues to do with relationships between business and the community.

3 From manufacturing to services

The economies of the industrialized nations of the world are undergoing radical restructuring at the present time – a restructuring not only as profound as that which took place at the time of the Industrial Revolution, but one which is taking place at a much faster pace. Alvin Toffler (1980) argues persuasively that the symptoms of this upheaval are generally misinterpreted by governments and their economic advisers who, in their efforts to prevent a collapse of the old economic order, are dealing with surface phenomena rather than the underlying structure where most change is taking place.

During previous periods of depressed economic activity in the industrial countries there have been crises in the great corporations, redundancies, plant closures, bankruptcies and rapid shrinking of major industries. But it was not the case that major new industries were growing rapidly at the same time.

Today the bulk of the traditional or 'smokestack' manufacturing industries, namely steel, automobile, rubber, textile and mechanical engineering, face serious problems. Yet at the same time the new 'horizon' industries of computers, electronics, biochemistry and aerospace, are thrusting ahead.

McDonald's has more employees than US steel. Golden arches, not blast furnaces, symbolize the American economy.

George F. Will

Clearly what is happening is not a recession but a restructuring. As a result of failing to understand this governments are tinkering with exchange rates, incomes policies, protectionist measures and interest rates all to no avail. In Toffler's terms we are shifting from a 'second wave' to a 'third wave' economy.

The new economic order has three distinguishing characteristics. First, it is a *service* economy, employing the great majority of the working population in service occupations. Secondly, the key resource of the new economic order is *knowledge*. Knowledge displaces capital, land and labour as the most important factor in wealth creation. Thirdly, the economics of the new society are no longer the economics of scarcity, they are the economics of *abundance*, of over capacity.

The service economy

In all the leading industrialized nations of the world, employment in the service industries has been increasing as a proportion of total employment while employment in all other industrial sectors has been in proportionate decline for the past two decades (longer in the case of the United States).

A generally accepted way of classifying economic activities is to group them under three broad headings – primary, secondary and tertiary. Primary relates to the land and the sea. It embraces agriculture, forestry, fishing, mining and quarrying. Secondary relates to the creation of tangible wealth from the raw materials and sources of energy and staple foods produced by the primary sector. It embraces all forms of manufacturing, construction and civil engineering. Tertiary – the 'service industries' – relates to the creation of intangible wealth. For example, areas such as education, health care, social services, financial services, travel, hotel and restaurant services, hairdressers, motor vehicle maintenance and repair, and entertainment.

Using this classification, Table 3.1 illustrates trends in occupational structure. With the United States leading the way, all the industrialized countries are experiencing the process which economists have come to describe as 'deindustrialization' of the workforce. The same trends can be seen in

Table 3.1
Shifts in occupational structure (1976–85)

		Total employed population (000s)	Employed in manu- facturing (000s)	%	Employed in service industries (000s)	%
USA	1976	88753	20261	23	57715	65
	1985	107150	20879	19	73521	69
Canada	1976	9477	1921	20	6104	64
	1985	11311	1981	18	7839	69
Netherlands	1976	4643	1105	24	2824	61
	1985	5106	990	19	3420	67
Australia	1976	5898	1282	22	3594	61
	1985	6646	1109	17	4413	66
Sweden	1976	4088	1100	27	2384	58
	1985	4299	968	22	2806	65
UK	1976	24492	7425	30	14087	58
	1985	24071	5728	24	15664	65
France	1976	21027	5740	27	10967	52
	1985	20941	4992	24	12372	59
Japan	1976	52710	13450	26	27310	52
	1985	58070	14530	25	32500	56
Italy	1977	19795	5444	27	9045	46
	1985	20507	4765	23	11315	55
Germany, Federal Republic of	1976	25059	8807	35	12119	48
	1985	25000	8009	32	13358	53
Spain	1976	12208	3177	26	4986	41
	1985	10315	2399	23	5218	51

the comparison of national output (or gross domestic product (GDP)). Even in Japan which is seen as an industrial super-power the proportion of GDP accounted for by primary and secondary industries has been falling since the early 1970s. In Japan by 1985 the output of the service sector accounted for over 55 per cent of GDP.

This process results from two interacting trends. The first is for the demand for labour in most primary and secondary industries to fall and the second is for the demand for labour in some service industries to rise.

The falling demand for manpower in the majority of the manufacturing industries has two principal causes. First, there is a shift taking place in the mix of industries making up the secondary sector. As more nations throughout the world become industrialized the old industrial nations lose their pre-eminence in the traditional, manufacturing industries which are also highly labour intensive. At first they lose export markets to indigenous production. Later on they lose a substantial share of their own home markets to cheap imports made possible by much lower labour costs in newly-industrializing countries. Industries typically declining in this way include textiles, leather clothing and footwear. These industries employed over one million people in the UK in 1971, but only just over half a million by 1985. The newer industries which develop and take the place of the old ones are typically much less labour intensive.

Secondly, technological progress in many primary and secondary industries results in productivity growing faster than output, with a consequent reduction in the demand for manpower. Industries in which there has been growth in output in the UK since 1964 accompanied by a significant reduction in the numbers employed include agriculture, electrical engineering, instrument engineering and food, drink and tobacco.

The fall in demand for manpower in the primary and secondary industries tends to accelerate during periods of recession and to be less pronounced or even absent altogether during periods of boom. Nevertheless the underlying trend is clear. Forecasts of the proportion likely to be employed in the primary and secondary industries by the year 2000 vary considerably, but given that in the UK in 1985 the proportion was 33 per cent, compared with 43 per cent fifteen years earlier in 1970, then a figure of 23 per cent would seem a reasonable indication of the likely position by the end of the century.

Demand for manpower in many of the so-called service industries, however, demonstrates a universal tendency to grow in all the advanced industrial societies. There are various reasons for this. There is, however, no common characteristic shared by the service industries which dictates that they should all follow the same trends. Indeed, the opposite is the case – employment in some service industries such as road and rail transport and domestic service has declined steadily.

Where the demand for labour *is* growing in the service

sector it is a reflection of one or more of the following tendencies. First, as a society grows more prosperous, and its living standards rise, members of that society tend to consume more and more services as part of a higher standard of living. For example, in the post-war era there was a growth in demand for holidays abroad, an increase in the frequency of eating out and the growth of personal banking. Secondly, the range and quality of services provided by governments tends to grow in line with economic growth, leading to enhanced employment in education, health and social services and in public administration generally. Thirdly, new consumer goods and new technologies bring into being new service industries or act as a stimulus to growth in existing ones. Thus the spread of ownership of motor cars leads to employment growth in a range of service industries – garages, drivers' clubs, and insurance companies.

Where demand for labour in the service sector is in decline there are four possible reasons. The first, of which the best example is domestic service, is that as wage levels rise some service industries characterized by low productivity growth price themselves out of the market. The second is that ownership of certain kinds of consumer durables enables people to provide for themselves services previously purchased from others. Examples are the motor car reducing usage of public transport, the washing machine reducing the usage of laundries, and television reducing cinema-going. Thirdly, the demand for certain types of servicing and repair occupations such as watch repairers declines as the cost of replacement items falls and it becomes uneconomic to maintain and repair them. Fourthly, in some service industries productivity growth has outstripped rising demand with a consequent reduction in numbers employed. The introduction of automatic telephone exchanges, for example, has led to a reduction in the number of telephonists despite very rapid growth in ownership and use of telephones.

The classification of economic activity into industry groups – primary, secondary and tertiary – creates a tendency to underestimate the extent to which we are becoming a nation of service workers. This is because there are millions of people engaged in service-type activities employed by organizations in the primary and secondary industries. These service workers make up a growing proportion of all workers in these industries, while the proportion of workers engaged in production declines. Because of the method by which industries and occupations are treated in the official statistics a catering worker employed in a factory canteen is classified under employment in manufacturing while a catering worker in a hotel is classified under employment in services. When the service workers in agriculture, mining, manufacturing, construction and the utilities are added to the workers in the service industries then the proportion of the UK working population engaged in producing services is probably in the region of 85 per cent and the proportion directly engaged in producing tangible goods is in the region of 15 per cent. Despite this, much of our understanding of the nature of work and employment is deeply rooted in the traditions and practices of directly productive work – exactly the kind of work that is disappearing rapidly!

Implications of a service economy

What are the implications of the trend towards a service economy? Before addressing this question it will help to clear up some popular misconceptions.

First, it is quite wrong to regard the primary and secondary industries as the wealth-producing industries and to take the view, as some commentators do, that the service industries do not create wealth, or even exist merely to consume it. Wealth can be defined as anything for which a need exists and in relation to which a market can be created. Thus access to education and health care or holidays abroad constitute processes of consumption of wealth just as much as ownership and use of consumer durables. Indeed the consumer acknowledges this when allocating disposable income and choosing between a new washing machine or a holiday.

Secondly, it is also wrong to assume that declining employment in manufacturing industry necessarily means declining volume of output of manufactured goods. Quite the opposite can happen (and indeed *must* happen if a country is to reach the stage of a prosperous post-industrial society). The same process has already happened in agriculture. Today's tiny agricultural workforce produces far more food than the proportionately larger farm labour force of the 19th century. The reason is, of course, productivity growth.

Thirdly, it is fallacious to believe that the service industries are dependent upon the manufacturing industries and can only survive in the presence of a strong manufacturing sector. Some service activities, it is true, are closely related to and dependent upon the continued existence of particular manufacturing industries or organizations, for example advertising in as far as it is concerned with promoting manufactured goods. But equally, certain manufacturing activities are closely related to and dependent upon the continued existence of particular service industries or organizations. For example, the manufacture of educational technology, hospital equipment, jumbo jets and automatic cash dispensers.

Fourthly, there is frequently misplaced concern about the ability of a nation in which the great majority of the working population are employed in the service sector to pay for its imports. There is no *necessary* connection between high service sector employment and balance of payments problems. Partly this is because of the point made previously – that a fall in manufacturing employment does not imply a related fall in manufacturing output. Partly it is because many service industries are capable of earning foreign currency through 'invisible' exports, for example tourism, banking, insurance, air transport and sea transport. This issue is discussed later in this chapter.

The restructuring of economic activity and the move to a service economy will have many important consequences, some of which cannot be foreseen at this early stage in the process. Among those which can be discerned, however, the following stand out as significant.

First, there is the increasing irrelevance of conventional ways of measuring economic growth. It is relatively easy to count up the number of bushels of corn, tons of coal or numbers of motor vehicles produced annually in a given society (although the process of placing a value on all the outputs of a society, applying a deflator to allow for inflation and then converting to a common currency via fluctuating exchange rates so as to compare the economic growth rates of different countries has always seemed to many to be a highly dubious process). How, though, does one build into the national accounts such things as an improvement in the quality of health care or the fact that people are increasingly better educated or even that there are twice as many world class symphony orchestras as there were ten years ago? What does follow is that those countries with a high proportion of economic activity created in the service sector will inevitably show an apparently lower rate of economic growth than countries in which the manufacturing sector is dominant. This undoubtedly explains part of the difference in post-war economic growth rates in the USA and the UK on the one hand (where they have been relatively low) and Germany and Japan on the other. It is beside the point to say that service industries are characterized by low productivity growth. It is rather that, for many service industries, productivity is an irrelevant and meaningless concept. Productivity could be increased in education by reducing the teacher/pupil ratio to 1 to 100 or in health care by reducing drastically the number of nursing staff per 100 beds, but of course this would do the opposite of what is understood as improving a service. In so many service sectors quality is all that matters.

From this it follows that eventually, if governments are to continue to attempt to monitor and manage economic performance, new ways of measuring increasing national prosperity will have to be found. Such measures must reflect improvements in the quality of life as well as changes in output of material goods.

Measurement of economic performance will, of course, be complicated by the fact that the cost of producing certain types of goods is falling and will continue to fall. To produce one million watches which sell at £25 each is to generate £25 million worth of wealth for society. To produce, ten years later, three million more reliable and more attractive watches which, because of drastic reductions in production costs, now sell for £5 each is, in fact, to have contributed significantly to the economic well-being of society. Yet, according to the conventions which govern our processes of economic accounting, output will appear to have fallen and only £15 million worth of wealth will have been generated.

A second important implication of the move to a service economy is that it tends to create pressures for growth in public expenditure, with a consequent rise in taxation to pay for it, and the growth of public bureaucracy. This is partly because some services can only be consumed publicly, in a shared way, for example policing, maintenance of the highways, air traffic control, and in consequence it seems right and natural that they should be publicly provided. It is partly because for reasons of social justice it is seen as desirable to provide certain services, for example, health care, social services, on the basis of need rather than ability to pay.

Some of the traditional thinking about the role of the public sector is increasingly being challenged as the scale of publicly provided services grows and the burden on the public purse enlarges proportionately. Increasingly a distinction is being drawn between *paying* for a service publicly and *providing* it by organizations located in the public sector. For example, refuse collection is paid for publicly via the rates but is provided increasingly by private contractors. The provision of certain services free of charge, irrespective of the individual's ability to pay, for example health care and education, is being challenged politically and by market forces as private educational institutions and private health care services are increasingly sought out by the more affluent groups in society seeking a better quality of service.

A further consequence of the shift to service sector employment which has profound consequences for the future of society is the growth in female employment at the expense of male employment. Whereas male employment in Great Britain fell by nearly one and a quarter million between 1975 and 1985 (a fall of 8 per cent), female employment increased by one half million (a rise of 4 per cent).

The jobs that are disappearing are for the most part traditionally the preserve of the male – in coal mining, the railways, shipbuilding, heavy and medium engineering and steel making. Employment growth has largely taken place in jobs where either men and women have enjoyed equal employment opportunities (such as clerical work, teaching, distribution) or in jobs where opportunities favour women (such as many office jobs, including word processing, and a wide range of jobs in the social services, in health care and in such industries as hotels and catering).

As job opportunities for women have increased, more married women have entered the labour force, swelling its numbers and thus inevitably making it more difficult for society to provide jobs for all those who are looking for them. Unemployment in Britain in 1987 (11.7 per cent in April) is at a very high level compared with some other countries but nevertheless Britain, together with the USA, provides more jobs for the population of working age, than any other industrialized country.

If present trends continue there may well be more women in employment than men in Britain and the US and some other countries by the year 2000. There will be four main types of household in consequence:

● The traditional pattern where the husband has a job and the wife/mother stays at home, looks after the children and acts as housekeeper. The proportion of households with this structure will diminish.

● The prosperous household in which both husband and wife have jobs.

● The newer type of household in which the wife is the chief earner and the husband is unemployed or has taken early retirement or is engaged in full-time further or higher education. The proportion of households of this kind is expected to grow rapidly.

● The single parent household in which a divorced or widowed woman or unmarried mother or divorced or widowered man supports a child or children by means of an income from employment or from social security. This type of unit is also expected to increase.

Gradually our concept of work will have to change to adjust to the changing structure of the economy and the changing composition of the workforce. Work has traditionally been a masculine preserve, characterized by being physically demanding, dirty and carried out in unpleasant, noisy environments. Whole branches of management practice, from work study to motivation theory have been based on this concept of the nature of work. Increasingly, work will become a female preserve, mentally or emotionally rather than physically demanding, carried out in clean, pleasant environments.

The balance of payments issue

Deindustrialization, as has been seen, has a number of causes. Among the most important, however, is loss of competitiveness, resulting in the decline of manufacturing output and employment as export markets are lost and imports penetrate the home market. This is a painful process and the natural tendency is to fight against it – to attempt to revive those industries in which it is occurring and to restore their competitiveness. To this end, whole industries are taken into public ownership, are given huge subsidies, guaranteed government contracts and given a measure of protection against imports. Despite such actions, industries such as steel, shipbuilding, motor vehicles and various branches of engineering continue to decline. The question then arises that if the decline is not arrested how will the country be able to obtain the foreign currency it needs to pay for its growing import bill. An often related question is how will the country earn enough wealth to maintain its standard of living, particularly bearing in mind its having to support a growing army of unemployed persons.

These issues have to be faced and the answers to the dilemmas posed must be woven into the pattern of the post-industrial society. Once again it must be emphasized that a post-industrial society is not a society characterized by a lower level of output of manufactured goods than an industrial society, any more than an industrial society is a society characterized by a lower level of food production than an agrarian society. The 'vision' of the post-industrial society is of one in which a steady growth of output of manufactured goods contributes both to a rising material standard of living and, because the goods being produced are in demand in world markets and are being produced competitively, to a healthy balance of payments. The industries producing such goods, however, are not necessarily the same 'smokestack' industries that have underpinned the great industrial economies. To a large extent they will be industries that have developed more recently, including such examples as electronics, aerospace, biotechnology and pharmaceuticals. As science and technology make further progress it can be expected that whole new industries will appear. These newer industries must largely take the place of the traditional older ones, both in wealth creation and in earning foreign currency.

A nation's ability to move ahead and become a successful and prosperous post-industrial society depends partly on its ability to develop these new industries by the turn of the century to the stage where they are able to make an adequate contribution to the balance of payments, either by creating new export markets or by substituting for imports in the home market. There are, however, two other important strategies which should guide industrial policy. First, it remains important to revive some of the declining industries and restore their competitiveness. The means of achieving this must be to make them face the full wind of competition rather than seek to protect them from it. Given skill and determination on the part of management and the rapid adoption of the most modern technology there is no reason why manufacturing industry in the USA and Western Europe cannot compete with the best in the world in both price and quality. In virtually every industry there are companies which demonstrate just this ability. The answer to declining competitiveness will not be found in nationalization, subsidies, or import controls but will depend on the quality of management in large numbers of individual enterprises.

The second strategy is to maintain and further develop the service industries' 'invisible' earnings. A nation's earnings of foreign currency other than by exporting manufactured goods are made up of a number of separate elements. The largest of these consists of the earnings of service industries – banking, insurance, other financial services, air and sea transport, tourism, professional services, etc. (Britain has a strong share in world trade in services and in 1985 its surplus from international trade in services was £5.8 billion.) Other elements include the remission of profits and dividends from overseas investments, and earnings derived from the sale of 'know-how' by means of patents and licences and from royalties.

To sum up, the balance of payments of a post-industrial society will involve a mix of exports and imports significantly different from those characterizing an industrial society. In the field of manufacture, high-technology goods – the products of the 'knowledge-intensive' industries – will play a much enhanced role in exports as will such service industries as those in the financial and professional services fields. There will be less scope for exports in the more traditional industries but in as far as they can restore competitiveness the growth of import penetration can be checked or even reversed.

Britain's prospects of achieving a satisfactory balance of payments situation with such a changed mix are founded on two favourable conditions. One is that foreign currency earned from North Sea oil provides a breathing space during which new industries can become established and grow. The other is Britain's relative advantage in the field of international trading of services. Factors working in the other direction include an industrial structure still strongly biased to the labour-intensive industries which create relatively little added value, and a capacity for resisting change which is unequalled anywhere.

Summary

The most evident aspect of the shift to a 'third wave' economy is the decline in the relative importance of manufacturing and the growth in the relative importance of services, both in terms of output and employment. This process is known as 'deindustrialization'. It reflects several trends – declining competitiveness of traditional labour-intensive manufacturing activities, the displacement of labour in manufacturing due to technological change and productivity growth and a rising demand for many services as a consequence of rising living standards.

At the same time the proportion of service-type occupations is growing within the manufacturing sector. Thus the nature of work is itself changing. In particular, more and more jobs are being created which are suited to the skills and qualities of women.

Other implications of the trend to a service economy include the need to develop new ways of measuring economic growth, pressures for increased public expenditure, and new opportunities for international trade in services.

4   The knowledge economy

As well as being a service economy the new economy is characterized by the fact that its central resource is *knowledge*, in contrast to the industrial economy where the central resource is *capital* or the agrarian economy in which the central resources are *land* and *labour*.

What is meant by knowledge in this context? Partly it means scientific knowledge in terms of the natural sciences – new developments in physics, astronomy, mathematics, chemistry and biology – and partly it means new knowledge about applications of science in such fields as engineering, electronics and medicine. But it also covers much knowledge of a non-scientific nature, for example the kind of knowledge needed by a successful investment trust fund manager, the kind of knowledge used by a psychologist to improve personnel selection techniques, the kind of knowledge used by a management consultant to improve a company's performance or the kind of knowledge used by an advertising agency to increase sales of a product.

Knowledge as a factor in production

This knowledge has a number of interesting characteristics which distinguish it from the factors of land, labour and capital. First, it cannot be consumed. If one person or institution uses some land or capital or the time of a labourer it is not possible for another person or institution simultaneously to make use of the same resource. Yet with knowledge this is possible – any number of persons or institutions can use the same piece of knowledge simultaneously, without in any sense depleting it.

Secondly, knowledge as property is much harder to protect than property in the form of land, slave labour or capital. Much of the knowledge which a firm 'possesses' is in fact stored in the minds of its employees and when they leave to join other organizations this goes with them. Patents are notoriously difficult to manage and safeguard. A country can export a great deal of knowledge via scientific papers in journals and at conferences yet see no return via foreign currency earnings.

Thirdly, it is extremely difficult to quantify the impact of knowledge on an economy. Economists can measure the crop yield from the land, the productivity of labour, the return on capital employed, but they have no instruments to tell how efficiently knowledge is being used. Stonier (1983) argues that the greatest challenge facing economics today is to find a way of answering this question.

The growing importance of knowledge as a resource has led to the recognition of the existence of 'knowledge-intensive' industries as distinct from capital- or labour-intensive industries and the key part played by 'knowledge' workers – scientists, engineers, technicians, computer programmers, software writers and indeed managers.

The extent to which an industry is knowledge-intensive can be approximately assessed by taking as an indicator the percentage of qualified manpower employed. Using such an indicator it can be seen that the shift from capital- and labour-intensive industry to knowledge-intensive industry is every bit as important in the process of transition to a post-industrial society as the shift in economic activity from manufacturing to services. Similarly, an analysis of shifts in occupational structure which distinguishes knowledge workers or information occupations shows that the growth in this type of employment is every bit as significant as the growth in service occupations.

The means by which knowledge is harnessed in the service of man is information technology, just as the means by which capital is harnessed is production technology – plant and equipment. The first steps in storing and disseminating knowledge involved the development of a written language and paper as a medium for storing it. In the 15th century, information technology took a giant leap forward with the invention of the printing press, enabling the same piece of knowledge to be reproduced thousands of times. Today we are still in the early stages of a much more significant stride forward – the revolution in information technology. Built around the microprocessor, it enables us to store vast amounts of information, to process it at incredible speed, to send it round the globe in a tiny fraction of time, all at an amazingly low and ever-decreasing cost.

Implications of a knowledge-intensive economy

What are the implications of the central role of knowledge in the post-industrial society? First, and most important, is the fact that the societies and corporations which will be most successful will be those which:

(a)   invest most in research and development and in education, particularly further and higher education;
(b)   prove most adept at finding applications for new knowledge and translating such applications into successful products or services in the market-place.

In every product there is a relationship between the amount of mass and the information that product contains. An ingot of lead has a high ratio of mass to information; a video cassette recorder has a high ratio of information to mass.

Paul Hawker (1984)

Secondly, as Daniel Bell (1973) points out, the key institutions in the post-industrial society are the knowledge-intensive institutions and there are some institutions which are more knowledge-intensive than any industrial concern, namely the universities and other centres of higher education. It follows that it is very important that close collaborative links be established between the institutions whose primary task is the creation and dissemination of new knowledge (the universities) and the institutions whose primary task is wealth creation (industry and commerce).

Finally, it is increasingly being recognized that when the material with which people are working is knowledge rather than iron and steel or chemicals or textiles they don't need to come together in one place in order to do their work. Provided they are in communication with each other to the extent that is necessary they can work at home or indeed while on the move or anywhere at all.

The competitive advantages on which our success depends all rest in the last resort on knowledge.

Knowledge has no marginal cost. It costs no more to use it in the 70 countries in which we operate than in one. This knowledge is of many kinds and a great deal of it is not patentable.

In every aspect of the business, knowledge is vital. Knowledge is not cheap. Around the world we spend many millions in acquiring it. But without this expenditure we could not survive against competition.

Dr Ernest Woodruffe
Chairman of Unilever, 1972

The exponential growth of knowledge

Fremont Rider the Wesleyan University librarian, quoted in Bell (1973) analysed the growth in the number of books in Yale University Library. Having calculated that on average the number of books in libraries of large American universities doubled every 16 years, he applied this figure to the case of Yale. In the early part of the 18th century there were about 1000 volumes in the Yale library. A doubling every 16 years would have resulted in a total of 2 600 000 books by 1938. In fact there were 2 784 000 by that date. In 1938 these were housed in some 80 miles of shelving and its card catalogue occupied something of the order of 10 000 drawers. A staff of 200 was required of whom half were employed in cataloguing.

If Yale Library continued to grow at the same rate by the year 2040 it would have 200 000 000 volumes on 6000 miles of shelves, catalogued in nearly ¾ million drawers. New material coming in at a rate of 12 000 000 volumes a year would require a cataloguing staff of over 6000.

The economics of abundance (the post-scarcity society)

The era of industrialization can be divided into two distinct phases – mass production and mass consumption. In the first phase, manufactured goods are produced in relatively small quantities, are relatively expensive and, indeed, in the case of many consumer goods are produced by the working classes for consumption by the middle and upper classes. The motor vehicle is one example, being produced for several decades by one class of person who came to work by bus, train or bicycle, for another class of person to use in connection with his/her profession or for leisure purposes. It has been pointed out that Henry Ford's great vision was not mass production but the coming of mass consumption. He foresaw the day when every American worker would own an automobile and had to invent mass production to make that dream come true.

Gradually, however, the problems of production began to be solved. Increasingly efficient machinery, improved working methods and new techniques of management brought about a revolution in productivity, making it possible to increase the real wages of workers, and reducing the costs of production of many items which, when produced in large quantities, now fell within the scope of the purchasing power of the average worker. As this transformation occurred, the problems facing society shifted away from how to produce things and on to the question of how to distribute them. The production management function declined in importance and status, the marketing function was born and grew up quickly. Advertising agencies attracted some of the best talent available in the service of the economy.

A similar process occurred earlier in agriculture. Again the transformation was from a state of relative scarcity to one in which supply and demand were in much better balance – by and large people were well-nourished and could afford to buy the food they needed. In agriculture, however, there was no stopping the growth of productivity. It quickly reached the stage in post-war Europe of over production, or over capacity, with a resultant potential collapse in prices that would have spelt ruin for the farming community. Many farmers would have been driven out of the industry via bankruptcy, the numbers engaged in farming would have contracted sharply, much of the land would have reverted to its wild state until a precarious balance between supply and demand was re-established. Even so the remorseless pressure of productivity growth, driving ahead faster than population growth and the demand for food, would have continued to depress prices. The answer invented by the Europeans to deal with this problem is called the Common Agricultural Policy. It involves protecting European farmers from competition from outside the EEC – whether from farmers with even higher productivity in Australia or New Zealand or from sugar plantation owners in the Caribbean subsidized by very low wages. It involves guaranteed prices for farmers which enable them to stay in business. It involves buying up excess production and either storing it in butter 'mountains', grain 'mountains' or wine 'lakes' or selling it off at low prices outside the EEC market, for example to the USSR. EEC bureaucrats who administer the Common Agricultural Policy have learned by experience the economics of abundance.

That experience has now increasingly to be applied to the manufacture of goods. Already productivity and capacity in many European industries have outstripped what the market can absorb. When the potential imports from countries with even higher productivity, such as Japan or from countries in the developing world with low labour costs, is added to this capacity it is clear that markets are more than capable of being saturated. Whether one looks at basic products such as steel, chemicals, man-made fibres or manufactured goods such as clothing and footwear, furniture, motor vehicles, watches, cameras, TV sets, washing machines, microcomputers, the answer is the same – over production and over capacity. Prices become depressed and gradually the least competitive producers are forced out of the market. There is (as yet) no common industrial policy analogous to the Common Agricultural Policy. In most countries (with the notable exception of Japan) local industries are exposed to the full force of overseas competition. Consumers enjoy the benefits of cheap goods and engage in conspicuous consumption, provided, that is, that they have managed to cling to a niche in the production system and have a job which provides them with the necessary income.

There is a story, no doubt apocryphal, of the president of a US automobile manufacturer showing a union leader the latest automated assembly plant. Pointing to the robots he said: 'What I like about them is that they will never go on strike'. 'No', said the union leader, 'but tell me, how many of your cars will they buy?' This little story encapsulates the problem perfectly. Increasingly the knowledge-intensive economies are capable of producing huge amounts of material wealth with the aid of only a small proportion of the population of working age – just as they can produce enough of the staple foods for their needs with the aid of less than 2 or 3 per cent of the working population. Given this increasing separation of the function of producing material wealth from the function of consuming it, how are people's claims to consume material goods to be settled? These claimants are of two kinds – those that have jobs, but whose work consists of providing services rather than goods and whose own productivity may be growing rather slowly, if at all, and those who have no jobs and under the present system must exist on a State handout.

For service workers in the private sector the question is settled by market forces. Very high real incomes are achieved by those whose service skills are relatively scarce and highly valued by society – medical consultants, barristers, pop stars and management consultants. Lower real incomes are earned by waitresses, refuse collectors, bus conductors and telephonists, but these lower incomes support a lifestyle which, in material terms, would have seemed middle class a few decades ago.

For service workers in the public sector the problem is much more difficult to resolve. It can be exemplified by taking nurses' or teachers' pay as examples. They obviously produce no material goods. Their salaries, however, will entitle them to consume a range of material goods and some services, according to their preferences and priorities. There seem to be two reasons most often advanced for not paying them higher salaries. One is that to do so would be inflationary. If the supply of goods were fixed, then to give nurses and teachers large pay increases would merely mean that their entitlement to a share of the available goods would rise and that the entitlement of other groups in society would consequently fall. Those other groups would quickly demand and obtain equivalent increases in salaries or wages so as to restore the status quo – but at a higher level of wages and prices, with no increase in real incomes. The other reason given is that pay increases for teachers and nurses increase public expenditure. This may be true in money terms, but if the inflation argument above is valid then the *proportion* of national income taken by public expenditure remains unchanged. A further possible reason for not awarding them higher pay is that most of the increased purchasing power would be spent on imports – thus creating balance of payments problems.

All three problems might be avoided by issuing each teacher and each nurse with a motor vehicle manufactured in Britain. It can be argued that to do so would not be inflationary since the increased demand could be met from existing capacity and would, through more efficient plant and labour force utilization, lead to lower rather than higher prices. It would not lead to an increase in government expenditure since the annual reduction in unemployment benefit and increase in taxation income would offset the capital cost of the vehicles. It would not lead to an increase in imports other than in respect of certain vehicle components purchased abroad. Such an approach will no doubt immediately be ridiculed by economists and politicians alike – which may well mean that it justifies further consideration.

The central issue facing policymakers and economic theorists as we move into the post-industrial phase is how to develop institutions capable of coping with abundance to replace our existing institutions which were born out of, and are based upon, assumptions of scarcity.

Beyond the boundaries of the advanced industrial nations there are hundreds of millions of people with a huge potential demand. The *physical* limits to satisfying these needs lie in the fields of energy resources and raw materials. These limits constitute far less of a constraint than was at one time believed. Far more formidable obstacles exist in the form of our economic institutions which have grown up on the basis that if people are to consume wealth they must play a proportionate part in its creation. Yet in a society in which increasingly the wealth is created not by people but by machines this time-honoured link breaks down.

There is no better mechanism than the market for allocating scarce resources. Once, however, resources cease to be scarce the market mechanism breaks down. This point can be illustrated by the sorry tale of what has happened to public transport. As more and more people have become car owners, demand for public road and rail transport has inevitably fallen. As the number of people travelling by public transport has declined, transport undertakings have struggled to maintain revenues by raising fares. Rising fares have caused yet more people to abandon public transport to buy and use their own cars. The result is a half-empty train from London to Birmingham beside a packed and congested motorway. The logical conclusion of this process is that the train eventually runs with only one passenger paying the 'economic' fare of £10 000! Naturally he declines the opportunity, the train is cancelled and eventually the line is closed down. The social tragedy is that the very people unlikely to have their own cars – the very young and the very old – are also the ones least able to afford the high fares.

What is the solution? One possibility lies in a radically new approach to consumption. When something is scarce then the price mechanism makes sense, since people with money to spend are choosing to allocate their spending power across a range of scarce resources. In the modern world, however, only some goods are scarce and others are produced in quantities in excess of demand (for example, cotton shirts, digital watches, ballpoint pens, butter). It is possible to envisage a situation in which the young, the unemployed, and pensioners are issued with vouchers which entitle them to consume according to need, for example EEC intervention butter, off-peak travel on trains and buses, certain necessities such as clothing and fuel. Indeed, society is now moving hesitantly towards such a solution, albeit with a fragmented approach, for example rail cards or free bus services for students and senior citizens and the allocation of EEC surplus butter to schools and old people's homes.

As has been seen, one of the most important consequences of modern technology applied to manufacturing is a significant fall in the real cost of manufactured goods. The fact that goods are becoming cheaper may be disguised during periods of high inflation but if a measure is used, such as the number of hours an average earner has to work in order to earn the sum needed to buy a particular good, then the decline in real prices becomes evident.

At the same time one of the most important consequences of rising living standards is a significant rise in the real cost of services provided by people. Higher wages for nurses, higher fees for doctors and lawyers are inevitably reflected in higher prices for medical care and legal advice since there is less scope for productivity growth in such service activities compared with most of manufacturing.

Over time these two trends are changing our patterns of consumption. When the services of people were relatively cheap because of low wages it was common for middle-class families to employ servants. Today's middle-class consumers cannot afford servants but they possess two cars, two or more televisions and several watches, cameras and similar goods. Increasingly the same applies to working-class households, at least in quantity terms; the cars may be smaller, the watches cheaper, the cameras simpler, but the characteristic remains one of conspicuous consumption.

The practice is fuelled not only by the relative cheapness of the goods offered and the power of advertising but increasingly by the availability of easy credit. The Access card is well named, since it provides access to the abundance society provides without having first to earn the income required. The principle of 'consume now, pay later' is not new. It has made home ownership possible for millions through the mortgage system. Its development in recent years, however, is of a different order and is changing the nature of our economic system in ways which are as yet difficult to define.

I believe that we have now left the economy of scarcity and scale, and are entering the economy of choice. Technology has made it possible to serve the needs of an increasingly diverse set of values and lifestyles among consumers and employees. Industrial-era technologies succeeded in creating an affluent society. Today, however, the organization success stories will depend less on massive concentrations of capital, technology and human resources on a single product or service in a stable market than on combinations of different skills and different technologies and different organizational arrangements serving different and highly segmented markets or needs.

William F. Miller
Managing Intellectual Organizations
SRI International, 1986

Summary

The central resource of the new economy is knowledge. As an economic resource, knowledge has three distinctive characteristics:

● It cannot be consumed in the way that capital and labour can.
● As property it is harder to protect than other types of resource.
● The impact on the economy is extremely hard to quantify.

As well as labour-intensive industries and capital-intensive industries there are knowledge-intensive industries. Their emergence is as important in the process of economic development as the shift from manufacturing to services.

In the next stage of economic development, success will accrue to those nations and to those corporations which invest most in research and development, education and training and which prove most adept at finding marketable applications for new knowledge.

It will be increasingly important for close links to be established between business and such knowledge-intensive institutions as universities. At the same time, given that the material people are working on is knowledge it will become less and less necessary for them to gather at the same place of work in order to do their jobs.

A further characteristic of the new economy is the existence of over supply and over capacity in many industries. Society is moving from an economy of scarcity to an economy of abundance.

New economic policies and mechanisms will be needed to eliminate unnecessary poverty and need in societies with the productive potential to more than satisfy demand for basic foodstuffs and manufactures. Similarly, new policies are needed so that excess productive capacity in the richer parts of the world can be used beneficially for the poorer countries.

5   Information technology

Information technology is playing the same role in the creation of a post-industrial society as energy technology (the steam engine, the electric motor, and the internal combustion engine) played in the creation of industrial society. It is transforming society in two principal ways. First, it creates new possibilities – the ability to manufacture new products and to provide new services. We already have pocket calculators, digitial watches, home computers, video-recorders, music synthesizers, and cellular radio. The future will bring us home banking and shopping, electronic funds transfer at point of sale (EFTPOS) and a host of other new products and services which we cannot yet foresee.

Secondly, technology changes our lives by its impact on productivity. Productivity gains in turn tend to have two sets of consequences. On the one hand, they result in a lower cost of production, and hence a lower price to the consumer, of the goods or services affected. This is why in real terms the price of such items as computers and watches has fallen so dramatically. On the other hand, a consequence which is less welcome is that where growth in demand and output cannot keep pace with the rate of increase in productivity, jobs are lost. This can lead either to the creation of a much needed supply of labour for a rapidly expanding economy or to mass unemployment in a stagnant or declining economy. This is true of all forms of technological change, but there are some distinctive features of information technology that need to be examined because of their implications for profound and radical change.

We may – and soon – have to rethink the way we look at economics and economies, and fairly radically. 'Information' is now classed as 'services', a 19th-century term for 'miscellaneous'. Actually it is no more services than electrical power (which is also classed under services). It is the primary material of an information-based economy, and in such an economy the schools are as much primary producers as the farmer – and their productivity perhaps more crucial.

Peter Drucker (1969)

The nature of information technology

What exactly is meant by 'information technology', or IT as it is now commonly called, and why is it so important? These are questions that are constantly being asked but not always satisfactorily answered. Satisfactory answers are to be found not in detailed technical knowledge of electronics systems and how they function, although some basic understanding of this is useful, but in a better understanding at a more philosophical level of what is meant by 'information' and its role, not only in work and wealth creation but in society at large.

All human activity, both in work and at leisure, involves processing information. Whether counting coins behind a bank counter, adding up the price of goods bought in a shop, playing a simple game of noughts and crosses, setting the type for the front page of a newspaper, reading a novel, learning a foreign language, controlling a 747 jetliner on its final approach to the runway, cutting a piece of metal to a precise shape or simply making a telephone call, people are performing essentially the same activity. Obviously, there are considerable differences in the complexity and difficulty of some of these tasks compared with others. There are also important differences in the code or language used in the process of performing them. Nevertheless, the basic activities are essentially the same and they are of five kinds:

1   *Input* – Information is taken in through the senses, mostly the eyes and ears but also through touch, taste and smell.
2   *Processing* – Doing things to the information: making

sense of it, if coded in plain language; decoding it if it is cryptic; if it is in figures performing calculations; if it is in a foreign language translating it. In all this people follow certain rules or laws – rules of logic, rules of grammar, laws of mathematics.

3 *Storage and retrieval* – Committing the information to memory, sometimes with conscious effort as when learning a part for a play or sometimes unconsciously as when years later people can still remember the plot of a novel. When the information is needed again, people retrieve it from memory, or at least try to – not always with complete success.

4 *Transmission* – Moving the information about. We move its storage location from the brain on to a sheet of paper, in words or by drawing a picture.

5 *Outputs* – Giving the information to others who need it or putting it out in other ways – for example, by carrying out control movements as when steering a car or using a welding torch.

Gradually over centuries, and with rapid innovation in the last 25 years, people have found more methods of transferring these information processing activities from human beings to other devices. This process has involved two quite distinct kinds of innovation. First, in the field of hardware as exemplified by such devices as the clock, the printing press, the telephone, the phonograph, the punched card sorting system and, latterly, the computer, space satellites and lasers. Secondly, in the field now referred to as software, we have invented language, the various branches of mathematics, various taxonomies, musical notation and codes such as Morse, and, most recently, various computer languages.

IT comprises this combination of hardware and software which makes possible the processing of information with little or no human intervention. The two main sources of innovation in recent years have been in the computer industry (particularly micro-electronic circuits (silicon chips) and simple programming languages such as BASIC) and in the telecommunications industry (particularly satellite communications and fibre optics).

IT brings a number of results which are regarded as advantageous, and superior to those achievable by human beings working without its assistance. These include:

1   Greatly enhanced *speed* of processing data.
2   Greatly improved *accuracy, reliability* and *quality* of information.
3   Ability to handle complex patterns of information (for example, as when playing chess) not at the level at which the most gifted human beings can operate but certainly at a level giving a *superior performance* to that which can be achieved by the average person.
4   Greatly *increased storage capacity* coupled with the facility to be able to retrieve instantly any single piece of information.

All of which adds up to the ability to carry out functions much more quickly, accurately and economically and, even more important, to additionally carry out that which previously could not be contemplated because of limited information processing capability.

The state of the art

The history of computing science is well known and will not be repeated here. Suffice it to say that there is general acceptance that current hardware and software systems represent the fourth generation in a series of major innovations following the invention of the first electronic calculating machines using thermionic valves during the Second World War. The most outstanding characteristic of fourth-generation systems is the extent to which they have broken down the boundaries between different forms of information processing activities taking place for the most part in different industries.

The hardware which has made this possible goes under a variety of descriptions. There are computers of various sizes in terms of processing power and memory capacity – mainframes, minicomputers, and microcomputers. These are increasingly linked into networks locally (local area networks) or distantly, together with other devices. Some of these are not obviously computers, for example word processors are computers disguised as typewriters or typesetters, electronic exchanges are computers disguised as telephone exchanges, synthesizers are computers disguised as keyboard musical instruments. Other devices include visual display units (VDUs), high-speed non-impact printers, cash dispensers and security locks. The hardware is supported by various types of software 'packages', the most commonly used of which are for databases, enabling vast quantities of information to be stored and retrieved; for spread-sheets, enabling financial information to be processed speedily and accurately; and for graphics enabling information to be represented visually, in colour and in three dimensions. In addition there is an enormous amount of specific software which relates to industrial applications (numerical control of machine tools), retailing applications (automated warehousing), and a wide range of applications in such diverse fields as medical science, war games, business simulation and architectural design.

The overall impact of all this technology is to break down the traditional boundaries which grew up between industries because they once used different and very specific technologies and in consequence required different kinds of skill in the people who worked in them. These skills were often of the kind which were built up during years of experience; thus movement of skilled personnel across the boundaries between industries was difficult, frequently impossible.

Increasingly today, and even more so in the future, different industries use the common technology of electronic information processing. A bank is no longer an institution which lends and borrows money, it is a system for processing information about credits and debits. As such its essential technology is the same as that of an insurance company, a travel agency, or a building society. In the same way a company which makes computers is creating information processing systems which are increasingly indistinguishable from the products of companies making telecommunications systems, word processors or electronically-based medical diagnostic equipment. The printing industry is increasingly being transformed into an industry which processes information electronically.

One result of this dissolving of boundaries will be a radical restructuring of industry. In the financial services sector this is already happening as banks, building societies, insurance companies and other types of institution take over each others' functions. It is also happening in manufacturing as companies which started life in such diverse fields as type-writers, computers, office furniture, photocopying, tele-phone exchanges, broadcasting and process control expand their activities to embrace all or most of these products. Increasingly, the only sensible answer to the question 'What business are we in?' is 'We are in the information business' – processing information (a bank), purveying information (a newspaper), or supplying information processing equipment (a computer manufacturer).

A second and related result is a remarkable collapse of the very highly specialized division of labour built up in society during the period of industrialization. Instead of bank clerks, insurance clerks, compositors, engineering craftsmen or warehousemen, information workers are needed – people who process information, using the same kind of equipment and the same skills regardless of the nature of the information beng processed. Information workers will, of course, be required at various levels. The highest grades will comprise the designers and developers of new hardware and software systems. Next will come the analysts and programmers who develop and apply the existing technology. Finally, there will be those who maintain the technology and those who operate it. Any or all of these will have skills capable of being transferred from banking to retailing, from retailing in turn to manufacturing; and from manufacturing in turn to printing or telecommunications, or indeed to any of a very wide range of industries.

Future developments

'Fifth generation' is the name given to a set of projects currently in hand in the advanced countries. Outstanding examples include the work going on in the ICOT laboratory in Japan sponsored by the Japanese Ministry of Industry and Trade, the US Government's DARPA programme, the UK's Alvey Programme, the EEC's ESPRIT project and IBM's own research programme (which may well be the biggest of the lot).

The term 'artificial intelligence' has been used with drama-tic intent (and effect) to describe the objective towards which these research programmes are directed. The debate as to whether or not computers can ever possess intelligence in the sense it is used to describe a quality of human beings can quickly become metaphysical and for the layman is more likely to confuse rather than illuminate. What is more important is to know what developments and applications can be expected in the future as a result of all this research effort, the main outcome of which will be to increase still further the processing power and memory capacity of computers while still further reducing the cost of computing.

The human brain contains, I am told, 10 thousand million cells, and each of these may have a thousand connections. Such enormous numbers used to daunt us and cause us to dismiss the possibility of making a machine with human-like ability, but now that we have grown used to moving forward at such a pace we can be less sure. Quite soon – in only 10 or 20 years perhaps, we will be able to assemble a machine as complex as the human brain. It may take us a long time to render it intelligent by loading in the right software or by altering the architecture, but that too will happen.

I think it certain that in decades, not centuries, machines of silicon will arise first to rival and then surpass their human progenitors. Once they surpass us they will be capable of their own design. In a real sense they will be reproductive. Silicon will have ended carbon's long monopoly. And ours, too, I suppose, for we will no longer be able to deem ourselves the finest intelligence in the known universe. In principle it could be stopped. There will be those who try, but it will happen, nonetheless. The lid of Pandora's box is starting to open.

Sir Clive Sinclair
From a report delivered
to the US
Congress, Washington DC
published in *Opinions*, September 1984

Some of the things we can expect are listed overleaf.

1 *Video communications* – first the picture-phone giving full colour vision, not only two-way calls but remote conferencing between three or more places. (Eventually holography will make full three-dimensional remote conferencing possible.)
2 *Mobile phones* – not today's car phone but a personal wrist-watch sized phone from which it will be possible to contact anyone anywhere.
3 *Interaction with VDUs* by voice recognition.
4 *Image transmission devices* which will compress data so that the 3.2 million bits necessary to send an A4 page of text will be reduced by a factor of 12 to 20.
5 *Programmable machines* (Robotics) in manufacturing capable of extremely flexible assembly work to tighter tolerances and extremely high quality standards.
6 *Speech compression devices* which will greatly increase the volume of communications traffic carried by a single telephone line.
7 *Computerized video-disc players* will virtually eliminate the market for static databases.

Not all the applications will be in work or in commerce. Professor Marvin Sirbu of the Center for Policy Alternatives, Massachusetts Institute of Technology has described a computerized game under development at MIT. Called *Star Trek* after the popular TV series, the game involves a number of players each of whom commands his/her own spaceship. On joining the game players choose, if they wish, to ally themselves with one of the many groups of players already in play. They sit at a display showing cockpit instruments and a star map. They can scan the area around their space-ship and view it on their screen; they can manoeuvre their own ship through space and engage in combat with other players. 'Phasers' and 'pluton torpedoes' are used in galactic warfare. Text messages can be sent to friend or foe and alliances formed or treaties broken.

A game such as this calls for a sophisticated terminal with considerable processing power and local storage capacity. Movements of spacecraft or launchings of weapons must be conveyed to all other players simultaneously so that their visual displays show the movements and actions of all players in real time.

This game is currently played on a local network with just a few players but there is no reason why the number of players could not grow to 100 or 1000 and be widely dispersed.

Such apparently frivolous applications of IT nevertheless have the power to transform the use of leisure time in society and to become the foundation of whole new branches of the leisure industry.

Philip Hughes of Logica sees clearly that the western countries, including the UK, are moving away from being industrial societies. Their future cannot, he believes, lie in manufacturing. It must lie initially with service industries and then with the knowledge-based industries of the future, which will be characterized by an intensive use of information technology. The implications are considerable. First, further education has to be seen as a necessity, not a luxury. We have to recognize that the uneven distribution of work – with a 40-hour week for the (shrinking) majority and unemployment for the (increasing) minority cannot endure and that work, and the wealth it creates, must be shared. This work will increasingly take place in and close to the home. Telecommunications will provide the infrastructure for the post-industrial society just as the railways provided it for the industrial society. The telecommunications network will be used for buying and selling, for learning and teaching, for meetings, for giving and receiving medical and legal advice, for consulting databases of all kinds, for all financial transactions including banking, and for entertainment.

Philip Hughes (1982)

Summary

IT involves the use of machinery (hardware) and codes (software) to make possible the transfer from human beings to machines of various information-processing functions such as entering, processing, storing and retrieving, transmitting and outputting data.

IT creates possibilities for new products and services and has dramatic effects on productivity.

Current IT systems are fourth-generation systems. They are breaking down the boundaries which previously existed between different industries and different occupations.

Future developments will come with fifth-generation devices. The impact of these on, for example, new products, productivity, product quality and the use of leisure time is incalculable.

Part Two
Post-Industrial Management

6 The new management

In what ways will management in the post-industrial society be different from management in industrial society? The answer to this question is a vitally important one for all who are concerned with selecting, recruiting, educating and training today's young managers who will become the strategic decision-makers of the post-industrial era.

Most frequently the answer is given in the form of lists of qualities or characteristics which future managers will need to a greater extent than was the case in the past. The trouble with such lists, which include such characteristics as leadership, vision, the ability to communicate, and interpersonal skills, is that they either refer to qualities of enduring importance (ones which were as important during the Roman Empire or the Renaissance or at the beginning of the Industrial Revolution as they are today) or, if they do refer to qualities which can be argued to be more important today, such as flexibility and the capacity to adapt to change or awareness of the environment, they are so obvious as to be scarcely worth mentioning. Furthermore, of what use is it to know that people will need to be more flexible in the future if it is not known how to identify flexibility when recruiting managers or how to develop it when training them?

A more productive approach would be to identify the ways in which managerial work is changing and consider what needs to be done, both to improve the process of selecting young persons with the abilities and aptitudes appropriate to the new tasks facing management and to train and develop them in the skills and techniques which will be required.

The nature of managerial work will not, of course, be totally and radically transformed as we move into a post-industrial world. There will, however, be very significant shifts in emphasis, in terms of both what managers are striving to achieve and the means available to them for achieving their goals. These shifts, which will move new issues to the centre of the stage, will be sufficiently significant to cause us to rethink our fixed images of the managerial process which have been built up during an industrial era which now belongs to the past. For example, concepts such as productivity (as defined in terms of output per man hour) play a central role in our traditional approach to defining the objectives of management yet cease to have any meaning in the context of the fully-automated manufacturing plant.

In Chapters 7 to 10 such shifts in emphasis are identified and each will be discussed in depth. They are briefly listed and commented upon here.

Service management

Emphasis is shifting from managing the production of tangible goods (raw materials, foodstuffs or manufactures) to the management of service. Obviously, organizations producing tangible goods will continue to exist in large numbers and will continue to need managing. Equally obviously, services have existed and have been managed since the beginning of civilization. What is significant, however, is, first, that in the post-industrial society the very large majority of managers (possibly up to 90 per cent) will be managing service-type activities (including many of those employed in organizations classified as belonging to the production industries) and, secondly, that the theories and models of management as contained in the literature and taught in the business schools have been built up very largely on the basis of experience in managing production.

The process of delivering high-quality, cost-effective service from large-scale complex organizations is, as a management art, in its infancy compared, for example, with what has been achieved in the field of the mass production of automobiles or consumer electronics goods or processed foods. *It is also a very different art*. There is a growing number of examples of organizations which have developed a reputation for being very good at it and it is important to find out what can be learned from them. They have developed their management systems internally rather than by building on a stock of collated and accessible knowledge. More significant is that the number of well known but *badly* managed service organizations in the US and Europe is legion. In terms of failure to deliver customer satisfaction cost-effectively most large-scale service organizations don't even begin to compare with the McDonalds restaurants or Marks & Spencers of this world and as and when they meet competitors who have developed sophisticated service management systems they will go out of business. Even state-owned monopolistic providers of service are not in the long run immune from this process. As has already been seen in educational and health services, citizens of increasingly affluent societies will find alternative sources of supply if they fail to meet their rising expectations. The growth in importance of service management and the need to learn how to carry it out more effectively is *the* most significant change that is taking place in the world of management.

Managing with information technology

The management of information technology is a totally different concept from technical knowledge of information *technology* which is a specialist's field and will not be discussed further. It is to do with the selection and arrangement of appropriate hardware and software into systems capable of supplying organizations with relevant and timely information in a cost-effective way. Enormous strides in information technology have made it possible to generate huge amounts of information very cheaply, to process this information very rapidly, to store it indefinitely in a very compact form, to retrieve it instantly and to move it to any part of the globe. Now it is necessary to learn how to use this ability to improve our effectiveness in managing organizations.

Managing talent

This involves a change in emphasis from managing labour and/or capital intensive organizations to managing knowledge-intensive organizations.

The knowledge-intensive organization can simply be defined as the organization which depends for its survival not upon an adequate supply of cheap labour, nor upon investment in modern plant and equipment but on its ability to develop and market superior knowledge. Examples include organizations in science-based industries, namely electronics, computer software, pharmaceuticals, agricultural research stations and biotechnology. However, the term 'knowledge-intensive' needs broadening and perhaps a better term is 'talent-intensive' because of the need to embrace within a common conceptual framework such industries and occupations as films, television, the arts, popular music, advertising, public relations, investment analysts, bond dealers, dealers in futures markets, sports clubs – indeed any organization which primarily earns its income by exploiting relatively rare human knowledge, talent, skill, aptitude, beauty, etc. The fact that such organizations may well employ quite large numbers of relatively unskilled workers and may simultaneously have quite substantial investment in plant and equipment should not be allowed to obscure the issue. The key test is what the customer is buying. For example, without the ability to attract the world's top tennis players all the capital invested in the All-England Lawn Tennis Club at Wimbledon would be a liability rather than an asset and none of the ticket collectors, catering workers, cleaners or clerical staff would have jobs. Wimbledon is in many ways a classic example of a talent-intensive organization. As a case study for management in the future it is much more relevant than General Motors or even Rank Xerox.

Managing cultural change

The transition from an industrial to a post-industrial society involves a cultural change (even a culture shock) both for societies and for the component institutions to do with community living, family life and working life. For some, the shock is too great and they collapse. Communities, as in the depressed regions of northern England, slowly disintegrate; the great industrial trade unions see their membership decline as rapidly as their power; and 'blue chip' companies, such as

Dunlop, St Gobain or Chrysler, get taken over, go into liquidation or have to be bailed out by governments. As citizens of societies in transition we are faced with massive changes in our own lives to which we have to adjust as best we can. As managers we carry the responsibility for helping organizations survive massive changes on many fronts simultaneously. The switch from a manufacturing to a service economy is undoubtedly the most fundamental change but this is linked systemically to a bewildering range of related changes including:

● The emergence of global markets and global competition in virtually every product or service field.
● The rapidly rising expectations of increasingly educated, articulate and sophisticated consumers.
● The equally rapidly rising expectations of an increasingly educated, articulate and sophisticated workforce.
● The possibilities offered by new technology for both product and process innovation.
● Increasing social pressure for new standards in respect of social responsibility, environmental protection, health and safety of workers and consumers.

The mature organizations which today still account for a high proportion of employment and wealth creation cannot cope with change on this scale without undergoing such radical change themselves as to merit the description 'culture change'. Founded in the last decades of the 19th century or in the first half of the 20th century in the context of an industrial society, they developed cultures based on the needs and characteristics of the societies in which they flourished. Cultures are notoriously hard to describe other than by listing their salient features. The ones that stand out are hierarchical, status ridden, bureaucratic, change resistant, inward looking, complacent, (even arrogant – sometimes noticeably so just at the 11th hour before collapse), male-dominated and production-oriented. These characteristics are found just as frequently in the large service sector organizations of the industrial era – the big banks, life insurance companies, the railways (particularly), even such relatively modern creations as the big airlines. These cultures are very deep rooted, very powerful and strongly resistant to change. Yet they must be changed, and in a lasting way.

Our training needs analysis, therefore, for the development of the post-industrial manager points to four requirements: to learn how to deliver service; to learn how to manage talent; to learn how to use information to obtain competitive advantage; and to learn how to manage cultural change. These are, of course, all interrelated. They represent the four key components of the typical organization of the post-industrial era – one which delivers a highly-competitive service package, which exploits human talent and know-how, which uses information strategically to obtain competitive advantage and which has successfully survived considerable cultural change.

7 Service management

The shift in emphasis in western economies from goods production to the provision of service calls for a radical transformation in the way organizations are designed, structured and managed.

Service has traditionally been associated with servility. As recently as 1986, Sir John Harvey-Jones, then Chairman of Britain's giant chemical concern, ICI, in referring to one of Britain's largest foreign currency earning industries, tourism, described its workers as 'a bunch of people in smocks, showing tourists around medieval castles'.

For the captains of traditional manufacturing industry, service meant something they were accustomed to receiving, not something they should concentrate on providing. Given that service itself is looked down upon it is not surprising that the quality of service offered by so many organizations is so poor. Yet today we are moving into an era of unprecedented growth in demand for the mass consumption of high-quality service. This explosive growth in demand is accompanied by major changes in the business environment facing service enterprises. These include:

● Deregulation   In the case of airlines and financial services, for example, deregulation removes constraints on competition, allows easier entry into markets, intensifies price competition, removes geographical restrictions on company operations, gives rise to needs for spe-

	cialization, differentiation and market segmentation and stimulates marketing activity generally, including the use of the mass media.
● Changes in professional standards	Making it possible, for example, for professional firms to advertise their services and to employ modern promotional techniques.
● Information technology	Permitting the 'industrialization' of service activities traditionally carried out locally and on a small scale; enabling new services to be developed (for example, electronic funds transfer at point of sale (EFTPOS); making possible more customer self-service (for example, automated teller machines outside banks) and leading to the development of centralized customer service systems (for example, hotel, airline or car rental reservation systems) and centralized customer records (for credit rating or for service calls).
● The growth of international markets	Services such as banking, insurance, travel, advertising and consultancy now involve global markets and global corporations.

By the year 2000 some 80 to 90 per cent of managers in western economies are likely to be concerned principally with the management of service. Yet by comparison with the management of goods production the literature on service management scarcely exists. This would not matter if the management of goods production and the management of service delivery were not radically different processes. In this chapter, however, it will be argued, and demonstrated, that the differences are great.

At this point it should be stressed that managing the delivery of service is not an activity confined to the service industries. The service element in manufacturing is becoming increasingly important as a factor determining competitive advantage. Consumer durables, such as cameras and washing machines, and industrial goods, such as photocopiers, are increasingly chosen for the reputation the maker has for service. Also, the distinction traditionally drawn between manufacturing and service enterprises often appears rather arbitrary and artificial. For example, is IBM today selling goods or its reputation for service? What about the modern printing corporation: is it in manufacturing, in that it uses factory machinery to process raw material and produce tangible goods in the form of books, magazines, brochures, etc? Or is it a service industry, concerned with processing an intangible product – information? Restaurants are classified as service organizations, yet they too use a considerable amount of machinery and process raw materials into tangible finished products.

Service management, without doubt, is an activity which is to be found in organizations of many different kinds, not just those confined to the service sector.

Services versus goods

How do services differ from goods, in terms of what the differences mean for the processes of management? Organizations which put strong emphasis on the delivery of high-quality service (no matter what category they are assigned to by government statisticians) are as different from traditional manufacturing organizations as the factory is from the farm.

There are seven key differences which, taken together, constitute a management process distinctively different from that involved in manufacturing:

● Intangibility   The intangibility of service has two important implications for management. First, it is not possible to put services into stock. This in turn causes considerable emphasis to be placed on matching supply and demand, and on smoothing fluctuations in demand so as to ensure optimum capacity utilization. Services cannot be stockpiled against periods of peak demand, and lost production (for example, due to strikes) cannot normally be recovered. Secondly, the intangibility of a service, together with the fact that quality control is much more difficult than in the case of goods, makes it impossible to show the customers, in advance of a transaction, exactly what it is that they are buying.

Because customers cannot send for a sample of a service, see one in a showroom or take one on approval, their choice of supplier is greatly influenced by the supplying organization's reputation and image, by past experience in dealing with that organization, by word of mouth recommendation, by the advice of experts (for example, *The Good Food Guide*) and 'guarantees' offered by trade associations such as the Association of British Travel Agents or the Automobile Association.

● The ephemeral nature of most service transactions

If improperly performed the service cannot normally be recalled or replaced. Compensation can be offered or another, virtually identical, service on another occasion but since each service transaction is unique such attempts to 'make good' often fall short of the mark. For example: a delayed flight resulting in a day's holiday lost: an overbooking, meaning a missed flight, or no hotel room for the night; an anniversary dinner for two by candlelight spoiled by a badly cooked meal; a computer error leading to a refusal of credit in embarrassing circumstances; a tooth extracted in error.

In order to attempt to avoid errors of this kind, quality assurance management must be more concerned with what happens *before* the service is delivered rather than with what happens afterwards, as is often the case with manufacturing (inspection and after sales service).

● Simultaneous production and consumption

Generally speaking, services are delivered where the customers are – they are not easily centralized. Large service organizations operate through branch networks. Service operatives are frequently beyond the reach and influence of supervision at the point of delivery.

● Human interaction

The personality, approach, manner, and cheerfulness of the service provider are essential parts of the service. Whereas it does not matter if the workers on the product assembly line look as if they are not enjoying making the customer's car, it matters enormously that the service worker looks as if he or she is enjoying serving the customer's drink, selling the customer a pair of shoes, or cashing his cheque.

This close interaction between the provider and consumer of a service means that the perceived quality of a given service is realized at what was described by Jan Carlzon of Scandinavian Airlines as the 'moment of truth', when the service provider and consumer confront one another. At that point of contact between the producer and the consumer what happens can no longer be directly influenced by the company. It is the skill and motivation, the attitude and knowledge of the person representing the organization interacting with the expectations and behaviour of the customer, which together will create the product. The functional distinction between production and sales is lost. Every frontline employee in a service activity is, inescapably, a salesperson.

This factor has two implications of the utmost importance. First, the key management task in a service organization is the selection, training and motivation of service personnel, coupled with the creation of a service-oriented culture running right through the organization. Secondly, it is the main source of the quality control problem in service management. Area managers of chains of shops or restaurants can call in to a local branch and check the layout of the merchandise or the quality of the soup. What they cannot check is whether the staff were smiling at the customers before they arrived or whether they will be courteous and attentive to customer needs after they have left.

● Customer involvement in production

It is frequently the case that successful delivery of a service calls for co-operative behaviour on the part of customers. Managers have to study how to manage their customers as well as their employees. This may involve educating customers to use a piece of technology such as an automated telling machine; persuading customers to conform with the organization's standards (for example, by wearing a tie in a restaurant); or getting customers to do part of the job themselves – self-service in a restaurant or filling station, for example.

● Specific applications of new technology

Organizations creating a service strategy for the 1990s must develop the capacity to think strategically about the potential of new technology. Traditionally, thinking has been conditioned to linking manufacturing with high technology and services with labour-intensive activities characterized by low technology. The information revolution changes this dramatically. Advanced technology has applications in so many service areas, for example transport and communications, financial services, retailing and health care. A new management approach is needed which can bring together the highest possible standards of concern for the customer as a person and the ability to make effective and economic use of the best that modern technology can offer.

● Female employment

In many service industries the majority of employees are women. This is even more the case in repect of 'frontline' personnel – receptionists, bank tellers, air hostesses, hairdressers, nurses, teachers, and shop assistants. Women do behave, as employees, in different ways from men. They are more likely, for example, to wish to work part-time or to have flexible working hours. Importantly, the organizations which employ them (hotel chains, banks, airlines, multiple retail chains, etc.) have been traditionally managed by men and have in consequence developed distinctively masculine cultures. Demands for equal opportunity are already bringing about changes in Britain (and more so in North America than in Western Europe) but a movement is certainly under way which will create an enormous demand for highly-trained senior and top level women managers in the next decade or so.

The special management problems of the service sector have been addressed by a number of writers whose work has been invaluable in preparing this chapter. A pioneer in the field is Richard Norman (1984) of the Service Management Group, a consultancy specializing in the management of service. In the US Karl Albrecht and Ron Zemke's work (1985) provides an excellent and wide-ranging review of recent developments, while most recently of all James Heskett (1986) of Harvard Business School has contributed invaluable concepts and insights.

In successful service enterprises, strategy is typically based on a clear statement of the organization's goals which, when communicated to employees, enables them to channel their efforts towards achieving competitive advantage. Such a clear and simple statement of service strategy and philosophy can position an organization in the market-place and pinpoint the market segment it is aiming at. Such strategic positioning is more difficult for a service organization than for a manufacturer whose products have visibly distinctive features and characteristics. Hotels, banks, building societies and estate agents can look very much alike to potential customers.

Examples of organizations with clear objectives and which are strongly positioned in the market include McDonalds restaurants, Holiday Inn Hotels, Marks and Spencer, Harvard Business School and Harrods. One of the best documented cases of an organization radically improving its fortunes by strategic positioning is the introduction in 1981 of the Euroclass by Scandinavian Airlines System (SAS), a service aimed exclusively at the business traveller and positioning SAS as *the* businessman's airline (see p. 77). By contrast, Woolworth in Britain which once had a clear position in the market has lost it in recent years and is in the process of struggling to redefine it.

In aiming at particular market segments it is important to achieve the correct balance between price and quality, in the context of the expectations that will exist in a particular segment of the market. For example, a particular segment of the business traveller market will be prepared to pay the extra fare to fly on Concorde in order to save time. Similarly, a guest at the Savoy Hotel London or the Mandarin in Hong Kong will be prepared to pay for the quality of service and surroundings that he or she expects. Yet in meeting the needs of a totally different market segment Virgin Airlines and McDonalds restaurants are equally concerned with quality and with meeting customer expectations, albeit at a radically different price level.

Segmentation can be carried further, particularly with the aid of modern information technology which not only makes it easier and cheaper to collect information about customer characteristics but also makes it easier to communicate with potential clients in a highly personal way. The combination of a set of preconceived standard packages each designed to meet the needs of one well understood market segment, together with highly personalized direct mail sales promotion can be very effective. Offers of financial services can be made, for example, to students, young married couples saving for their first home, homeowners, parents of school-age children, retired people and so on. Each piece of direct mail sales promotion carries the appearance of having been designed individually for the recipient.

Understanding customers' needs and expectations

The key to success in marketing services lies in full knowledge of the needs, expectations and attitudes of customers.

● Customer feedback is the one essential type of management information. In a service organization it can be a remarkably cheap source of market research. Most large hotel chains and some tour operators invite their customers to complete questionnaires and rate various aspects of the service delivery (although it is often surprising how badly these questionnaires are designed). But when were you last asked to assess your bank, your local supermarket, your nearest hospital? The customer who isn't asked his or her opinion eventually expresses it by voting with his or her feet.

● The customer needs and expects 'customer friendly' systems rather than ones which are designed to meet the convenience of those who operate the system or are merely designed without much concern for people – whether customers or operatives. (An example of 'unfriendly' systems encountered recently include an application form for insurance for people over 55 years of age with such small print few people of that age would be able to read it with or without the aid of spectacles.)

● It is not enough to *give* good service, customers must *perceive* that they are getting good service.

- The customer is not concerned with and cannot be bothered with the problems facing the organization. Staff shortages, computer breakdowns, power cuts, or strikes are the manager's problems and they cannot be offloaded onto the customer.
- Customer loyalty can be built to the level where it is relatively durable, but its strength does tend to vary according to the nature of the service, and it is not a factor common to all services. People tend to be more loyal to their banks than to their dry-cleaners, for example. Even where customer loyalty is relatively strong it can quickly be destroyed by a failure to meet expectations.

What service benefits are your customers looking for?

- Friendliness, courtesy, being treated like VIPs
- Punctuality, speed of service, no queues, etc.
- Cheapness, no frills
- Consistency, reliability
- Quality, the best that money can buy, luxury
- Choice
- Absence of 'hassle', everything taken care of, no worry
- Safety, security
- Excitement, thrills, adventure
- Confidentiality
- Flexibility, the ability to tailor service to individuals
- Status
- Attractive, clean, bright surroundings

- When considering the purchase of a service, potential customers have to make judgements on criteria other than the quality of the service itself since, unlike a product, it does not yet exist. These other criteria might include impressions gained from other users of the service, from the way the service is promoted or 'packaged', the type of premises from which the service is provided, and, above all, the type of people employed to deliver the service. Where possible they may try to sample the service before making any commitment, for example by testing a travel agency's efficiency by seeing how quickly it can supply accurate information about a place they would like to visit.

● Customers notice when the standard of service falls below their expectations but they also notice when it rises above them. The rose in a vase in a hotel room with a welcoming note from the manager costs very little but because it exceeds expectations it can have a disproportionate effect on customer satisfaction levels.

● Attitudes which have been built up over several years to be favourable can be destroyed by a single experience of bad service.

If a company that is supposed to be operating in a service industry has a department called the 'customer service department' what are all the other departments supposed to be doing?

Karl Albrecht and Ron Zemke (1985)

The SAS story

In 1981 Scandinavian Airlines System (SAS) was struggling, as were most of the world's airlines. Its results showed an $8 million loss. A new chief executive, Jan Carlzon, was appointed at the age of 39. He took the company from a lossmaking situation to a profit of $71 million on sales of $2 billion in just over a year. SAS was also voted 'airline of the year'. How did he do it? Quite simply, by improving the service to the customer – by putting the customer first. His great achievement, however, was to create awareness of and enthusiasm for the concept of service at every level and in every location in an organization employing 20 000. He did this by a combination of visionary leadership, exceptional powers of communication and intensive training programmes. At the same time, at the conceptual level he studied the nature and needs of the market and developed a package for business travellers which earned for SAS the reputation of being 'the businessman's airline'.

The sayings and teachings of Jan Carlzon are many and varied. The most important is 'We have 50 000 moments of truth out there every day'. A 'moment of truth' is any episode involving interaction between a customer and a representative of the company which gives the customer an opportunity to form an impression of the organization.

Managing service operations

The key to success in managing service operations lies in achieving the right balance between efficiency and cost control on the one hand and delivering the quality of service which matches customer expectations on the other.

Efficiency and cost control
Efficiency and cost control can be improved by a variety of methods. One approach is to 'industrialize' the service. There are three ways of setting about this.

1   By using technology as a substitute for human involvement (automation). For example, automatic teller machines, luggage X-ray machines, automatic highway toll collectors, coin-operated car washers.
2   By improving working methods in a systematic way (rationalization). This covers a wide range of activities involving human service operations following carefully defined procedures which are simultaneously economic and provide customer satisfaction. (Frequently the speedier the service the lower the cost *and* the greater the customer satisfaction.) Examples range from cleaning a hotel room to completing the sale/purchase of a house.
3   By limiting the range of variability in the service (standardization). For example, restricted menu restaurants like McDonalds, packaged tours, unit trusts.

Given high labour costs an obvious way of reducing the overall cost of a service is to increase the proportion of self-service. A key question for service managers is, therefore: 'How can I make my clients more productive for my operation?' The most important inducement is probably cost. Clients will act in ways which save money or result in getting more value for money. But beyond that, participation can be made an interesting or even exciting experience. A self-service retail store can offer a number of advantages. It may take more time and involve more physical effort, but it gives a wider range of choice and an opportunity to learn about what is available. Some people are even happy when less social interaction is involved. For example, many people much prefer to operate self service petrol pumps rather than to interact with forecourt attendants. Sometimes, in order to involve clients, it is necessary to give some formal education or training. This is common among service-oriented product companies like IBM and Xerox, who spend a great deal of money on customer education. But briefer shorter guides on how to behave and what to do are given in a much less formal way to customers in a wide range of service organizations.

Some of the questions that Richard Norman (1984) has suggested should be asked in relation to managing clients are as follows:

1   Can we influence the timing of the customer's demand?
2   Do the customers have spare time while they are waiting when they could do something and then not be bored?
3   Is there unnecessary face-to-face contact between clients and our employees?
4   Do we use such contacts to maximum effect?
5   Are our employees doing repetitive work which customers could do themselves?
6   Do clients sometimes try to get past the contact personnel and do things themselves and should we allow them?
7   Do customers show interest in and knowledge about the tasks of contact personnel?
8   Do we find a small minority of customers who disturb the service delivery system and spoil its effectiveness?
9   Do the customers ask for information which is available elsewhere?
10 Can the customers do more work for each other?
11 Can part of the service delivery process be relocated? For example, to decrease the cost of premises.

Improving efficiency needs to be considered carefully in order to find approaches which do not damage quality. It is particularly important to avoid anything which can be perceived as an assembly-line or 'sausage machine' operation.

Delivering a service frequently involves a series of events or interactions rather than a single transaction. Even a simple meal in a restaurant may involve being received by one person, being served a drink in a bar by another, giving your order for food to a third, for wine to a fourth, being shown to your table by a fifth, actually served by two more and settling your check with a cashier before finally being helped into your coat by the cloakroom attendant. Staying in a hotel can involve a much longer chain of interactions. Some propositions can be put forward about such sequences:

1   The strength of the chain is equal to the strength of its weakest link. One failure to perform at any stage can destroy the total experience.
2   The more people involved the less likely the customer is to find the experience rewarding. This is partly because (as with the sequence of operations on the factory assembly line) bottlenecks and delays occur during the process which cause the customer to become bored and frustrated. It is also partly because the more people dealing with a single customer the less likely is each to treat that customer as special. (In all my years travelling by air I have only once been spoken to by an airline employee who used my name – the airline was Cathay Pacific.)
3   Such sequences are usually based on strong task specialization among the service personnel. Thus the barman in the restaurant is unable to get the customer a menu. The waiter is unable to bring the customer the bill. This is organizationally and administratively rational except that it overlooks the fact that the customer doesn't know the intricacies of the organization's structure and division of labour. He or she expects a response from the organization as a whole from the nearest service employee.
4   Frequently the customer has no idea who is in charge of the operation – whom to complain to when things go wrong or praise when things go well. Sometimes this is because there *is* no one in charge.

Quality control

In service management quality is all important. Quality is the source of customer satisfaction, the factor which determines the extent to which consuming the service meets his or her expectations.

In managing quality it is useful to adopt a distinction made by Richard Norman (1984) between two elements that exist within the total service package – the core service and peripheral factors. For example, the service package which consists of a night's accommodation in a hotel is made up of a core element and peripherals. The core is what is regarded by the customer as essential in meeting his or her needs and will probably include physical elements such as a comfortable bed and a bathroom and intangibles such as courteous reception, cleanliness and peace and quiet. The peripherals will also include physical factors such as a trouser press or a mending kit and intangibles such as a courtesy limousine service from the airport.

The process of improving quality can involve improving the core service or adding or improving peripherals, or both. It is important to note, however, that yesterday's peripherals are part of today's core service and today's peripherals will become part of the core service in the eyes of the customer of the future. This process can clearly be seen in the hotel business as more 'extras' have come to be taken for granted by the customer. This reflects a general tendency for the process of raising quality to result in raising expectations with the consequence that the standard of quality can never again be lowered.

Good service management gives extremely careful consideration to the nature of the physical setting within which that action takes place. The design of the interior of a hotel or restaurant and the message communicated by that design and the atmosphere that it suggests are all critical components of the service delivery system. Whether the service is delivered in the retail outlet or is brought by a van to one's own home, or mediated through a machine like an automated bank teller or a simple telephone, design is a key element in service management.

Service management involves some contradictory elements. On the one hand quality assurance in service management, even right at the very top, calls for extreme attention to detail. The general manager of a first-class hotel will need to be in touch with the most minute detailed component of the service the hotel is providing, even down to the choice of cutlery and table linen. At the same time, given the social nature of the process which goes on in the hotel, it will only succeed if individual members of hotel staff have room for individual judgement and freedom of action. It will only work if *spontaneous* behaviour can take place at the level of the receptionist or porter.

The managing director of a large hotel chain telephoned one of the hotels in the group and told the manager he would be visiting the hotel for dinner a few days later, bringing one guest. When the time came the meal and service were faultless – from the beautifully arranged flowers on the table, through each separate course, the immaculate service of the wine, the excellence of the coffee, the proffering of the choicest cigars and rarest liqueurs. After the meal the chief executive asked the hotel manager to join him for a while and introduced his guest as the group's new personnel director. He then asked the following question: 'Tell me, did you go to considerable trouble to see I was particularly well treated or did all the diners here tonight get the same standard of food and service?' He then added – 'Before you answer let me tell you that if you say you didn't arrange anything special I shall want to know why the hell not, but if you tell me this was special treatment I shall want to know why all our customers over there are getting second best'.

The manager thought briefly before replying. 'You had exactly the same treatment as our other guests tonight – that is to say the best possible food, wine and service that my staff and I can provide'. He got the answer right and confirmed his chief's belief that he was due for promotion.

Human resource management

Customers, when dealing with a successful service company, are overall made aware of a special kind of attitude present in every employee who interacts with clients, an attitude which says 'we are here to serve you and that is what gives us satisfaction in our work'. Thus, managing quality cannot be separated from managing and motivating people.

Personnel selection
Good service-oriented companies tend to put enormous effort and care into screening and selecting their staff. Never-

theless, there is still considerable lack of expertise and knowledge in this area and a need for more concepts, and new and more sophisticated management tools. Service companies must market themselves not only to their clients, but also to their employees. Indeed, for long-term success the service company must fulfil a genuine function in respect of personal development of its employees.

One problem that needs to be solved by a new approach to personnel selection is that a great many service jobs, while not requiring very high level formal academic education or technical skill of the kind that is examined in the modern educational system, may nevertheless be extremely demanding in other ways – for example, handling very difficult and delicate situations carefully, and demonstrating what might be described as social intelligence. Quite often service employees are required to exercise a great deal of judgement, initiative, tact and even wisdom and often have to do this in a situation in which they cannot call on their superiors for assistance. There is a need to develop tests and measures of social intelligence or factors such as initiative, judgement and capacity for spontaneous action to help improve selection procedures.

Education and training

The next important component of the delivery of the service is, of course, education and training. The best service companies organize their own schools for this purpose. McDonalds restaurants have their own impressive 'Hamburger University' and IBM runs one of the largest educational operations in the world. Although one of the tasks of such institutions is to teach the technical skills needed in the business, there is much more to their education and training programmes than this. It is very important that employees learn various interactive skills. Some airlines, for example, provide their cabin staff with training in transactional analysis to help them cope with difficult and demanding clients. Many companies use role play and conflict simulation as training tools. Some even advertise the fact that they have such educational programmes thus communicating to the customer the nature and quality of their service delivery system. At McDonalds the staff learn to have eye contact with every customer and this training certainly seems to work.

It is of course important not to rely on education and training programmes by themselves. They have to be followed through and they have to be given full support from top management. Finally, it has to be seen that the top management are behaving in the same ways that are recommended by the training programmes.

Motivating service personnel

The people closest to the job are those who know it best. They can most easily see where the scope for improving the quality of the service lies and, if there are changes to be made, they will have to carry them out.

In many service companies the frontline people are treated as the *least* important in terms of pay, status, training and career prospects.

Highly-motivated service personnel are easily recognized both by their customers and their managers. Yet most managers don't know how to create a strong motivation to serve and in consequence when it is absent they have very little idea how to set about creating it. For service personnel to be highly committed to their task they need:

(a) to be reasonably satisfied (but not necessarily 'over the moon') about their own pay, status, working conditions, etc.;

(b) to receive regular, frequent feedback from the customer as to the perceived quality of service provided;

(c) to receive adequate recognition (financial and non-financial) from their own management when their performance justifies it;

(d) to feel they are strongly supported in their frontline role by other personnel in the organization at all levels;

(e) to genuinely feel that their own top management puts the customer first – and that they are there to serve the customer and *be served by* the management;

(f) to feel that service is a team operation, that they belong to the team and that it is a winning team;

(g) to have the confidence that comes from having been properly trained for the job.

When these conditions are met, service employees give good service, customers are grateful, smile at them and thank them. This in turn reinforces motivation and a virtuous spiral is created. By contrast, many organizations suffer the vicious circle of poorly-motivated staff, poor service, angry frustrated customers and even lower staff morale and motivation.

The great advantage of service sector management is that in a well designed, well delivered service activity, both the client and the employee emerge from the process of delivering the service with an enhanced sense of well-being and self esteem. They both feel better for the experience.

Summary

1   The shift in emphasis from goods production to the provision of service calls for a radically new approach to management.

2   The need for better service management is particularly important in view of such factors as deregulation in such industries as air transport and financial services, growth of competitiveness in many professional fields of activity, the impact of new technology and the growth of international trading in services.

3   The differences between service management and the management of production include the intangibility and ephemeral nature of services, the fact that production and consumption occur simultaneously, the important part played by human interaction, the involvement of the customer in the production process, specific applications of new technology and the high proportion of female employment.

4   A strategic approach to marketing service is important. This involves positioning an organization clearly in its market and identifying the market segment it is aiming at, and achieving the correct balance between price and quality which will match the expectations of that market segment. Vital elements in this are knowledge of the customer base and feedback about customer experience.

5   In managing service operations a balance must also be struck between efficiency and quality. Efficiency can be increased by 'industrializing' service and costs can be reduced by introducing a greater degree of self-service. In doing so, however, great care must be taken to avoid damaging the quality of the service.

6 Quality can be improved either by raising the quality of the service itself (the 'core service') or by adding or improving extras or 'peripherals'.
7 The most important route to quality lies through managing and motivating service personnel. This involves personnel selection, education and training and reward systems as well as good leadership.

8 Managing with information technology

Where is the wisdom we have lost in knowledge? Where is the knowledge we have lost in information?

T.S. Eliot

The manager's task falls into two distinct types of activity – dealing with people and processing information. Technological progress will have relatively little impact on the way the first is carried out, but it will revolutionize the way the second is performed.

Information technology (IT) will make it possible for managers to have much more information processing carried out at much lower cost and in much shorter time. IT will affect the quantity and quality of the information; the nature of the channels through which it is transmitted; the speed with which it can be sent over great distances; the form in which it is presented; the way it is stored; and its accessibility.

Given the possibilities created by advances in IT, the danger is that managers will be so overwhelmed by data and so confused by a bewildering succession of technological innovations that they will end up in a state of paralysis, incapable of positive action. It is vitally important that they should approach IT, therefore, from the viewpoint of the needs of the business, concentrating upon how to use it to gain competitive advantage, and that they should not allow their decisions and choices to be technology-driven.

One British company which has successfully used IT to gain competitive advantage is Thomson Holidays. Colin Palmer, Thomson Holiday's deputy managing director says 'technology has become the basis of our business'. Thomson's investment in technology has enabled the company to outperform its competitors in the tour operators' price war. On 3 November 1985 the company's computers handled 3291 bookings in the first few hours of business at almost one a second, while other firms' systems ground to a halt under an avalanche of enquiries. Thomson's aggressive marketing strategy is dependent for its effectiveness on its ability to handle mass bookings. IT in such cases, is clearly a strategic resource, one enabling the company to secure competitive advantage.

Another example is the development of the electronic banking service 'Homelink' by the Nottingham Building Society, which shifted the Society from being just one more medium-sized provincial savings institution to becoming a nationwide financial service network. Sadly, these examples are exceptions. A study sponsored by Britain's Department of Trade and Industry carried out in 1984 by consultants A.T. Kearney revealed that IT inspires either anxiety or apathy in most boardrooms. The survey covered 2325 firms and showed that few of them attempted to exploit IT strategically. Another survey by the Pactel consulting group found that chief executives looked on IT as a tool for achieving productivity growth rather than as a means of gaining competitive advantage.

American examples of the appropriate use of IT include Merrill Lynch, which launched its cash management system back in 1978. This combined banking services which were traditionally separate, such as lines of credit, cheque, investment and equity accounts, into a single monthly statement with idle cash being automatically moved into a high interest account. This new service attracted $1 billion in the first year. By 1986 the company was managing assets of $85 billion and still had over 70 per cent of the market for this type of service.

American Airlines was the first US carrier to offer an on-line reservation system to travel agents. Its 'Sabre' system has been taken up by 10 000 of the 24 000 US travel agents using computerized systems – 40 per cent more than its nearest rival. Sabre lists flight schedules of over 400 airlines but gave American Airlines a competitive edge by displaying its flights first. Also the company charges other airlines $1.75 for each booking, bringing income estimated at $170 million in 1985. This is an example of a market in which it is vital to be ahead of the competition – only four other US carriers now find room in the market for an on-line reservation service.

Types of IT application

IT has five distinct types of application:

1 Where the organization's product consists of information. Examples include education, publishing, entertainment, and advertising. IT can enable a better product to be delivered at lower cost.
2 Where the basic product or service is not information but where added value can be created by building IT into the product or service involved. Examples include computerized control and monitoring systems in automobiles, programmable control systems on domestic appliances and automatic cash dispensers in banking.
3 Where information processing activities are involved in producing an organization's output – whether goods or services. These activities are usually referred to as process automation, factory automation or office automation.
4 Where information activities are involved in monitoring the achievement of the organization's tasks. These are usually described as management information systems (MIS).
5 Where IT can be used to generate new products or services, that is product innovation.

Not only can IT be used to improve organizational effectiveness in each of these areas, it can, by integrating information arising under each of these headings greatly improve the functioning of the organizational system as a whole. IT applications of a strategic nature will be considered under each of these headings.

Information as product

Under this heading there are many examples of using IT strategically so as to obtain competitive advantage. Here we are considering instances in which the customer is buying various kinds of information – news, weather forecasts, share prices, company information, information about ranges of goods available and their price or quality, information about research findings in a particular scientific field – the list is endless. The customer will be attracted to use a particular source of information for any number of reasons: it is accurate, frequently updated, easily accessed, cheap to access, easily understood, is attractively packaged, offers a wide range of choice (for example, several TV channels) and so on. Strategic use of IT in respect of any particular information service must first involve being quite clear about what it is that the customer is buying, what is most important – price, speed of response, quality, packaging or whatever. Given firm conclusions on this basic issue, consideration can then be given to using IT so as to more effectively meet the needs of the customer and thus gain competitive edge. Examples include the following:

● Printing local versions of newspapers such as the *Wall Street Journal* or the *Financial Times* simultaneously in different countries.

● Providing share price movements and other financial data on-line and in real time.

● Offering consumers additional TV channels via cable services or satellites.

● On-line abstracting services covering scientific journals.

● Use of interactive video for training programmes.

Using IT to add value
In this area it is vitally important to be 'market-driven' rather than 'technology driven'. Do drivers really want cars that talk back to them in synthetic voices when they fail to engage their seat belts? Will the additional element in the product or service provided by IT be seen as a genuine customer benefit or a gimmick? Even where it is seen as a genuine customer benefit, can people be persuaded that it justifies a premium price? Is the IT involved capable of being used by the customer without considerable investment in customer education? What are the after-sales service implications and costs of IT add-ons? The golden rule in this area of application is that the most effective IT add-ons are those which enable the basic product or service to do more effectively the job it is designed to do or which attracts the customer to wish to own or use it. Examples include systems which make it

possible for cars to operate with greater fuel economy and safety, control systems which result in the more effective *and* more economic heating of buildings, controls which cause domestic appliances of all kinds to do their jobs to high performance standards with a minimum of human supervision, applications which free the users of financial services from previous constraints of time and place (for example, cash dispensers and credit cards).

Process automation

In this field of application managers must ask some basic questions.

● What information processing activities are involved in the operations I am responsible for? These can be grouped under main headings:

(a) Information which specifies the nature of the product or service (plans, designs, drawings, syllabuses, etc.).
(b) Information involved in controlling the actual production of the product or service. (Control information, in the case of machines; a wide range of types of information in the case of service-type operations, for example information about a patient's heart beat and breathing during a surgical operation.)
(c) Information about the movements of things, whether they are components on a production line, trains in a railway network, or bank transfers.

● How are these activities being performed currently? In particular, which aspects are performed by technology and which by human beings?
● How could they be performed using the most up-to-date IT systems available so as to reduce costs, improve quality, improve delivery times, thus giving my company competitive advantage?

Process automation in manufacturing

The term advanced manufacturing technology (AMT) has evolved to describe a whole set of applications of automation covering all stages of manufacturing. All the technology is available now and has been proven in use. It includes:

● Computer-aided design and manufacturing (CAD/CAM)

- Computer numerically controlled machine tools (CNC)
- Flexible manufacturing systems (FMS)
- Robots
- Automatic guided vehicles
- Automated materials handling and warehousing

Investing in AMT takes both time and money and such strategic investment decisions cannot be justified other than in the context of a strategic plan for the business. A much deeper understanding of this process is needed among the institutional investors, stock market analysts and financial journalists who react so strongly to half-yearly accounts. Undoubtedly much of the success of the Japanese reflects their greater ability to take a longer-term view of company performance. One of the key tasks of top management is to convince investors to back companies operating on a programme of strategic investment and to steer clear of those which are not. Investing in AMT, done wisely, will improve competitive edge by making it possible to produce better quality products, in greater variety, at lower cost, with shorter lead times.

The choice of technology and the establishment of priorities must reflect the firm's competitive position in its markets which in turn will determine what is most important – quality, ability to customize products and produce variety economically, cost reduction, reduction in working capital or quicker response times. It is vital not to be 'technology-driven'. For example, it might appear sensible to invest in a highly-sophisticated automated system for storing and handling materials and bought-in components. Yet the whole storage problem might be better (and much more cheaply) resolved by adopting a 'just-in-time' delivery system.

Process automation in retailing
Modern retailing operations involve very large numbers of transactions, of enormous variety, carried out at great speed. The scope for using IT to process the vast amount of information involved is considerable. Currently, attention is focused on four main applications – electronic data capture at point of sale, electronic funds transfer at point of sale (EFTPOS), teleshopping and automated warehousing.

Electronic data capture at point of sale is an application of IT that has been undergoing development for many years. The long lead time is a function of the need to agree standards and procedures between retailers, manufacturers and suppliers of IT equipment internationally. There now exists, however, an international electronic article numbering system (EAN) expressed in bar code form. This code is incorporated in the packaging at the manufacturing stage and includes information about the identity of the item. The same information, together with the selling price is entered by the retailer into the store computer. When a customer picks the product and takes it to the checkout the cashier passes it across a laser beam which records the code. The checkout terminal passes the information to the store computer which feeds back the product description and price which are displayed for the customer and printed on the customer's receipt. (Currently only a few hundred stores in the UK are using this system but the numbers are growing rapidly.)

The most important advantage for the retailer is the gain in information which enables staff scheduling to be improved to meet fluctuations in customer demand and thus diminish checkout queues, and which makes it less likely that the store will run out of stock of any particular item. Labour is saved in that it is not necessary to price each item of stock individually.

The electronic transfer of funds at point of sale (EFTPOS) involves the direct debiting of a customer's bank account (either immediately or at agreed settlement dates) in respect of sums spent in stores. The main advantages of this system are expected to be a large reduction in losses due to cheque frauds and, as a result of a quicker throughput of customers, a reduction in the number of checkout operators.

Teleshopping is in its infancy but is expected to grow rapidly in the next decade or so as an alternative to mail order shopping or as a facility for the elderly, the disabled, those living in remote areas, or those who find visiting the shops an unpleasant experience.

Automated Warehousing: Huge savings both in labour costs and space costs have been and will continue to be achieved in computerized warehouses and distribution depots where goods are located by computer so as to optimize the use of the available space and orders are picked by computer for delivery without involvement of warehouse staff.

Office automation

The word 'office' is used loosely in practice and can refer to a building housing thousands of white-collar employees involved in processing data for a service industry such as banking or insurance or to a small glass-fronted section of a manufacturing workshop to which the foreman occasionally retires to do paperwork. For the purposes of this chapter the term is used more in the former sense to refer to the 'factory' or 'operations centre' of a business organization in the service industries (or in central or local government) and in which the production workers are in effect clerks, typists, and other white-collar workers.

The role of information technology in this type of office of the future is likely to pass through three stages:

1 *Office mechanization.* Current common practice is for manual or mechanical processes carried out in the office to be replaced by the use of electronic equipment. Much clerical and secretarial work is replaced by word processors, electronic filing systems and electronic mail. This can be seen as the modern equivalent of moving from hand tools to power tools.

2 *Office automation.* Here the emphasis is placed not on the low level clerical/secretarial functions but on the purpose or 'mission' of the office and how it can best be achieved – whether it is to issue driving licences, approve insurance claims or check claims for social benefits. Such an approach involves designing hardware configurations and software specific to the office's primary task. It is analogous to the shift from machine tools to computer-managed manufacturing systems.

3 *Information systems.* This approach carries the logic of IT to the ultimate and sees the office as a place in which information is assembled and used for decision-making purposes. The decision-makers will have access to internal and external databases and will be provided with software which includes the means for modelling the business and asking 'what if' questions. The result would be a much more flexible, responsive and 'organic' approach than that described in the previous paragraph.

Management information

Before considering the implications of IT for management information systems it is useful first to emphasize what management information is for. Basically, it supports two important management functions – *control* and *decision-making*. Managers need information to enable them to exercise control over what is going on in the organization, for example how sales are going, what is happening to costs, what was the response to the last recruitment advertising. Armed with such information they can monitor the organization's performance and identify areas where changes will effect improvements. They also need information on which to base their decisions. Information about trends in costs, in inflation, in competitors' prices and strength of demand will be vital in reaching pricing decisions, for example. Information about the state of the order book and customer requirements will be important in deciding whether or not to authorize overtime. Managers are as dependent on information as deep sea divers are on their oxygen line. IT makes it possible for them to be endowed with information well beyond what would have seemed possible 10 or 20 years ago.

The role of IT

Information technology cannot work magic. It cannot, for example, make available information that simply does not exist. If no one has yet researched the market for fine English porcelain in Venezuela, all the on-line databases in the world will still not be able to furnish the would-be exporter with useful information. It can, however, achieve the following:

● It can make information available much more cheaply than previously. Thus,
● It can make available information which was not previously accessible to managers because of cost considerations.
● It can provide digested information – information which has already been analysed and processed, abstracted or summarized so as to provide the manager with the key facts.
● It can present this information in many different formats – printed or on screen, in the form of text, figures, graphics and, in the not too distant future, in the form of the spoken word.

● It can provide information much more quickly than previously – in real time, if necessary.
● It enables large amounts of information to be stored *and* to have instant access to any of it.
● It frees the manager from having to carry out managerial work in a particular office location.

Faced with such possibilities, and having in most cases very little knowledge of the opportunities opened up by modern technology, many managers fail to take advantage of the situation. Instead they passively accept the stream of information directed at them by functional specialists, such as accountants and production managers, who, in the absence of any strong leadership and direction from line management, have adopted the standard procedures available via packaged software and well-proven hardware systems.

The more effective approach is to start at the other end of the chain with the managerial task, and for the manager to begin by asking and answering questions such as the following:

● What information is essential if I am to do my job properly?
● How quickly after the events it relates to do I need to have this information?
● How frequently do I need to have it?
● In what format will it best suit my purpose and my way of processing information? (Some people are enlightened by charts but blinded by figures, for example.)
● What costs am I prepared to incur in order to get this information service?
● What analyses do I wish to be carried out on the information routinely?
● What further analyses do I need to be able to authorize from time to time?
● What part of the information will I need to keep – and for how long?
● What information will I need to pass on to others in order to do my job properly and to help them do theirs. How can I do this with the minimum expenditure of time and money?

It is this kind of questioning process which is most likely to lead to the successful exploitation of IT in support of management information systems. In looking for the answers it is important to be aware of and to avoid the most common mistakes. These include:

● Confusing data with information.
● Not starting from the basis of a conceptual model of the business as a system and in consequence having no clear idea as to what constitutes key management information.
● Over-concentration on recording history rather than setting up early warning systems to help plot the future course of events.
● Over-concentration on short-term data closely related to the bottom line – sales, cost of sales, overheads, net profit, cash flow, etc. and overlooking vital information about the longer-term health of the organization as reflected in the attitudes and behaviour of employees and customers.
● Over-concentration on information about what one's own organization is doing – neglecting the competition.

Spawning new products and services

The final role of IT in the business is to create competitive advantage by exploiting it so as to create new products and services. Examples include retailing organizations developing their own highly-profitable financial services operations to provide consumer credit and then building further financial services on to the base thus created; the floating-off of in-house software departments to become free-standing computer software consultancies; the development of a seat reservation system by one airline, initially for their own use but then made available as a highly-profitable service business to other airlines.

The basis for such innovations is twofold – the notion that information has value and that it can be sold without having to relinquish it, and the idea that IT makes it very much more likely than in the past that information can be economically and profitably packaged for mass distribution.

The strategic use of IT – an integrated approach

Michael Porter and Victor Miller, writing in the *Harvard*

Business Review (1985), discuss the strategic deployment of IT to gain competitive advantage and give special emphasis to the way in which it can be used so as to optimize the total business system, not just its individual parts. They introduce the concept of the 'value chain' – a series of linkages between the various activities carried out in a company.

They identify nine types of activity which form part of this chain and argue that each of them must either be performed at a lower cost relative to competitors or at a quality level high enough to warrant a premium price. The nine activities are grouped into five 'primary' activities and four 'support' activities, as follows:

Primary activities
● Inbound logistics
● Operations
● Outbound logistics
● Marketing and sales
● Service

Support activities
● Firm infrastructure
● Human resource management
● Technology development
● Procurement

Because of the linkages between these activities, the way one is performed can affect the cost or effectiveness of other activities. Linkages also give rise to potential trade-offs, for example using better raw materials leading to a reduction in after-sales service costs. Linkages create a need for co-ordination. Smooth co-ordination can reduce inventory and speed up delivery time.

The company's value chain is part of a wider system which includes value chains of its suppliers, distributors and customers. Linkages exist not only inside a company but between the activities of a company and those of its suppliers and distributors. A company can create competitive advantage by paying attention to these. For example, a confectionery manufacturer persuades its supplier of chocolate to deliver it in bulk liquid form rather than in solid blocks. 'Just-in-time' deliveries is the most frequently quoted example.

Each activity creates and uses information of some kind. For example:

● Logistics – schedules, routes, transportation rates.
● Service – call schedules, parts used, labour costs, data on product failure.

Porter and Miller suggest the desirability of assessing what they call the 'information intensity' of the activities in the value chain. Information intensity can arise from such factors as large numbers of customers or suppliers, large numbers of components and parts, the number of distinct product varieties, a large number of steps in the production process. They suggest that investment in IT will give the best returns in the areas of greatest information intensity. The greatest returns, however, are likely to be those which exploit the linkages, both those between the different activities taking place within the company and those with suppliers, distributors and customers.

Rockart and Scott Morton (1984) quote a good example of this in the case of the US company Foremost McKesson. The firm is a distribution company with a history of modest performance. After a change in the chief executive a new approach to the use of IT was adopted. Every step in the value chain was examined with a view to executing each one as efficiently as possible. In particular areas considerable savings were achieved. For example, in purchasing, computers were used to develop more accurate forecasts of demand for different products; in goods inwards, incoming items were checked against invoices; inventory was reduced. The most effective application, however, was that which exploited linkages with the company's customers. Terminals were installed in the drug stores which took the company's products, allowing them to enter orders directly. The drug stores benefited from prompt delivery but at the same time Foremost McKesson's costs were reduced. As customers began to ask for new lines the product range was expanded to include them. Because the customers' staff had been trained to operate the terminal and were practised in its use, customers were reluctant to switch to an alternative supplier. Foremost McKesson also found out that its customers often claimed on a third party (usually a health insurance firm) for payment for some of the products supplied. They offered to collect these funds, a process which not only saved the drug store a job but speeded up McKesson's cash flow.

Summary

1 IT offers great possibilities for increasing organizational effectiveness if used strategically so as to gain competitive advantage.

2 There are five main areas of application:

(a) *Information as product*. IT can make possible the simultaneous reduction in cost *and* improvement in quality which provides a competitive edge.

(b) *Information as added value*. IT can be used to provide add-ons which enable the basic product or service to achieve more effectively or economically the job it was designed to do.

(c) *Process automation*. In factory, office and shop IT can be used to specify the product or service, to monitor and control its actual production and to keep track of the movements of things.

(d) *Management information systems*. Providing managers with accurate and timely information for control and decision-making, economically, in the manager's preferred format and readily accessible wherever he or she may be.

(e) *New product development*. Exploiting the growing recognition that information has value and that IT makes it possible to package it for mass distribution.

3 IT can be used so as to optimize the total business system, not just its component parts. This involves a strategic approach based on a conceptual framework which identifies the linkages between the main activities of a company. These are:

Primary activities
- Inbound logistics
- Operations
- Outbound logistics
- Marketing and sales
- Services

Support activities
- Firm infrastructure
- Human resource management
- Technology development
- Procurement

9 Managing talent

As was seen in Chapter 4, in a world over-supplied with cheap labour, with huge sums of capital seeking investment opportunities, the one resource which remains in short supply is knowledge. The highest living standards and the greatest achievements will accrue to those countries best able to identify, nurture and exploit innovative knowledge of all kinds, as well as other intangible resources which, like knowledge, are developed and possessed by rare, talented individuals.

The implications of a knowledge-based economy for the process of management were clearly seen by Peter Drucker as early as 1969. Quoting Kuznet's classic study of growth in the US economy he pointed out that it was new knowledge rather than additions of capital and labour which caused productivity growth. It not only led to productivity growth in established industries, but created entire new industries with new technologies. It did so as a result of the effective management of knowledge.

Drucker, urging the need for an economic theory which related knowledge inputs to outputs, a theory which would lead to measurement of the effectiveness of applied knowledge, the output of 'knowledge industries' and the effectiveness of education and training, was concerned chiefly with the macro or societal level. The same need exists, in the form of a theory of managerial economics, at the micro or enterprise level.

Following Drucker many other writers, notably Bell (1973) and Toffler (1980) have elaborated and emphasized still further the role of knowledge in the modern economy. Despite this, acceptance of the idea has been remarkably slow in coming. Policy decisions at both national and corporate level are still taken on the basis of often implicit but nonetheless outmoded assumptions which place undue emphasis on the importance of capital and labour as economic resources. Even more so, ordinary people in their roles as managers and workers, consumers of goods and services and as parents advising their children on educational matters think and behave in traditional but increasingly inappropriate ways.

The need for a radical shift in conceptual frameworks exists, therefore, right through western industrialized society – not only among managers and employees but also among consumers, educators, politicians and (perhaps most of all) economists. The point can be illustrated in many ways – the following is just one example. When a car starts to function poorly – it won't start in the mornings, or it is using too much fuel, or it is cutting out when idling – the owner, unless he is an expert mechanic, will take it to a service station. He does this because he believes that the service station employs people who possess superior *knowledge*, who are capable of correctly diagnosing the cause of the trouble and can put it right. Yet when the job is done, and he gets the bill, he is charged for parts and *labour*, at so much per hour. If the mechanic is poorly trained and not very knowledgeable, and as a result takes several hours to do the job (and even then does not do it perfectly), the bill will be correspondingly high. The customer will normally pay without too much argument, however, since like everyone else involved he sees 'labour' as the commodity he has purchased (rather than *knowledge*) and is prepared to pay for the quantity he has consumed. If, however, he had taken his vehicle to a different service station, one employing an extremely well-trained and competent mechanic, who was able to diagnose the cause of the problem in a few minutes and rectify it immediately, and with *perfect* results while the customer waited, the probability is that the customer would ask 'Do I owe you anything?', implying that he expected to pay for *labour* but not for *knowledge* and that as the quantity of *labour* was extremely small there should be no charge.

The same outdated way of looking at things will be reflected in the status and rewards system at the service station.

Its ability to attract and retain its customers depends primarily on the skill and knowledge of its mechanics. Yet in terms of pay and status they will often rank lower than office personnel dealing with routine paperwork, receptionists and sales staff. The rational response of the able mechanic to this situation will be to start his own business. The more rational customers will then beat a path to his door. The rational responses on the part of the service station management might include the following:

● Give as much attention to the selection of mechanics as to the selection of managers – test their diagnostic ability, their competence in handling tools and equipment, their general level of intelligence and their personal qualities. Screen for problems such as alcoholism.

● Invest in regular training so as to ensure the mechanics' knowledge remains abreast of developments in vehicle design.

● Treat the front-line employees, the mechanics, as what they are – the firm's most important assets. Pay them accordingly, give them staff status, good working conditions and facilities.

● Feature the mechanics as personalities, highlighting their experience and qualifications in promotional literature – in the same way a restaurant might feature its chef.

● Invest in appropriate diagnostic equipment, power tools and other technological aids to efficient servicing.

● Sell its services not on a per hours labour basis, as a commodity, but in terms of a price for a particular result achieved or activity carried out.

Wealth from knowledge – a classic example

The idea of producing high-quality clear flat glass by floating molten glass on to the surface of a bath of molten metal, cooling it while still on the metal and then passing it through an annealing oven to produce a flat, high-finished continuous ribbon of glass without grinding or polishing, was that of Mr Alastair (now Sir Alastair) Pilkington in 1952. The British patent was applied for in December 1952 and the patent was sealed in July 1957. A US patent was issued in November 1959.

Early samples of the glass were made in a pilot plant in 1953. The first production plant started operations in 1957 but it was not until 1958 that the first satisfactory glass was produced. By this time the company's investment in the process had reached £3 million and £7 million had been spent on development by the time float glass production could replace all the firm's traditional plate glass production facilities.

At the time of the first successful commercial production of the new glass Pilkington's Board recognized that the company would not be able to exploit the full potential of the process worldwide from its own resources, so it was decided to license the process. There are now (in 1986) 35 licensees of the process, operating 108 float glass plants in different parts of the world, and further licences are under negotiation.

By 1985 annual sales of flat glass exceeded £1 billion and contributed £83m of the Pilkington Group's trading profit of £87m. A further £30m profit contribution was derived from licensing income and technical fees.

Broadening the knowledge concept – the 'talent-intensive organization'

Both Bell (1973) and Drucker (1969), however, in giving such strong emphasis to the centrality of knowledge in the post-industrial society, have singled out only one element among several which will increasingly become the sources of wealth creation. Knowledge, however broadly defined, so as to include scientific knowledge at one end of the spectrum and marketing 'know-how' at the other, is undoubtedly a vitally important resource; but so are other things created by talented individuals – entertainment, works of art, designs for clothes or buildings. The post-industrial society is better described as a 'talent-intensive' society rather than as one which is 'knowledge-intensive'. Its wealth-creators are not only scientists, engineers and technologists of all kinds, but also professional sports players, musicians, artists, pop stars, architects, fashion designers, interior decorators, investment analysts, university teachers in all disciplines, landscape gardeners, heart surgeons, writers, lawyers and accountants. Alongside such knowledge-intensive institutions as universities, research laboratories, software houses and high-technology manufacturing plants, the key wealth-creating institutions include architectural practices, firms of accountants, lawyers and management consultants, merchant banks, design studios, television production companies, publishers, professional sports clubs, and advertising agencies.

Whereas, in the past, talented people worked mainly as individuals or joined together in small partnerships, today's talent-intensive organizations can employ thousands of people, can be global in scope, and have annual turnovers in billions of dollars.

Organizations of all kinds, and not just ones which are particularly talent-intensive, can create greater added value or achieve competitive edge by making their traditional operations more talent-intensive. Clothing and footwear manufacturers can do so by placing greater emphasis on design and advertising. Restaurants can do so by hiring outstanding chefs. Department stores can increase market share by employing highly-talented window-dressers and merchandisers.

Managing the knowledge- or talent-intensive organization involves learning not only a new set of skills and techniques, but also a new set of attitudes. The field is largely uncharted and it is impossible to do justice to it within the confines of this chapter. Two aspects, will, however, be treated, even if only for the purpose of raising key questions and stimulating others to develop more precise and comprehensive answers to them. These two aspects are, first, managing and motivating knowledge workers or highly-talented personnel and, secondly, accounting for knowledge or talent as a resource.

Managing and motivating knowledge creators and talented personnel

The first requirement is for the manager of the knowledge- or talent-intensive organization to recognize it as such and to understand that without an adequate supply of talent the organization has no future, regardless of its level of financial reserves, the value of its fixed assets or its current price/earnings ratio.

The manager must then develop strategies for the achievement of the following important objectives:

1 Recruiting an adequate supply of young entrants with the potential to become highly-talented performers.
2 Developing that potential by training and coaching.
3 Retaining the services of a high proportion of those recruited and trained in this way.
4 Recruiting, if necessary, an adequate supply of already trained and accomplished performers – and retraining them.
5 Motivating the talented personnel both to achieve high levels of performance and to build strong ties of loyalty to the organization.
6 Searching for ways of maintaining and raising the productivity of the most talented personnel.
7 Ensuring that everything possible is done to prevent 'poaching' and 'stealing' of talent and knowledge to competitors.

Acquiring and retaining talented employees

The 'labour market' for talent is increasingly an international one. Whether one talks about top-level scientists and engineers in aerospace and computers, consultant surgeons, tennis stars, pop singers, investment analysts, fashion designers, chefs or professors of English literature, they are in demand everywhere in the world. Conventional national standards in terms of salaries and terms and conditions of employment are increasingly irrelevant in this context. Failure to face this fact, both nationally and at the level of the corporation, has resulted in a significant flow of talent from countries with generally lower living standards to countries with generally higher living standards – the so-called 'brain drain'. So the first lesson, in managing talent, is that the total reward offered by the employing organization must increasingly be competitive *on a global scale*. The alternative is to be slowly starved of talent and to lose the ability to compete.

The phrase 'total reward' is significant here. In the case of highly-talented people this means more than signing on fees, high salaries, stock options, top-hat pension schemes and the like. It also extends to opportunities for personal and career development; the quality of life for the whole family not just the employee; freedom and autonomy on the job; and other factors. An extremely important self-reinforcing factor is the prestige and reputation of the employer in its own field. Top US academics can be persuaded to spend part of their career at Oxford or Cambridge University, despite lower salaries compared with the USA, while it would take a very large reward package indeed to attract a leading British academic to an obscure campus in the southern part of the USA. In the same way, Covent Garden can attract the best opera singers, Wimbledon the best tennis players, BBC television the best producers. What is less certain is how long Rolls-Royce can continue to attract the best aircraft engine designers or whether ICL or any other UK-based computer company can compete effectively for talent with IBM.

Motivating talented personnel
Motivational factors are generally of even greater importance when dealing with highly-gifted personnel than when dealing with the normal workforce. Drucker (1969), for example, describes the conflict between the traditional view of the knowledge worker and his position as an employee. The scientist working in a large company's research laboratory is clearly not a labourer yet his status is that of an employee. He cannot be told precisely what to do or how to do it, as in the case of an unskilled or semi-skilled worker, yet he will have a 'boss'. Frequently his boss will not belong to his discipline and will not fully understand the nature of work. Yet he will be appraised by him and must accept broad guidance and direction from him.

Richard de Lange, managing director, industrial relations, of Philips, the Dutch electronics group, describes the process of changing very rapidly 'from a company of workers into a company of intellectuals'. The top of the company's organizational pyramid was continually broadening while the base was becoming narrower. In 1985 Philips recruited 2000 people with higher education qualifications in Holland alone and would exceed this number in 1986. Also, in 1985 they had recruited 150 people of high academic quality from outside Holland – taking people, for example, from Ireland where there were excellent universities but few jobs.

De Lange points out the problems involved in developing work and career patterns which strike a balance between the expectations of highly-qualified 'knowledge workers' and the basic tasks which had to be carried out. The company was amassing large numbers of highly-trained people in research centres and somehow had to achieve there the same improvements in productivity as they had in the factories. The company's ability to remain competitive would depend more and more on the speed and effectiveness of its innovative processes, while the relative importance of its industrial activities would lessen.

Graham Turner (1986)

Collectively, the employed educated middle classes who constitute the knowledge workers are today's true capitalists in that through their pension funds they own a large part of industry. Yet individually they are dependent on their jobs for security, status and income. This state of dependence is in conflict with their self-esteem as knowledge professionals. Where insensitive management sharpens this conflict, highly-educated young people become quickly disenchanted with their jobs. This is why they protest against the 'stupidity' of business and seek careers in the professions or universities.

We will have to learn to manage the knowledge worker both for productivity and for satisfaction, both for achievement and for status. We will have to learn to give the knowledge worker a job big enough to challenge him and to permit performance as a professional.

Peter Drucker (1969)

Knowledge workers need to be challenged to achieve. They require that demands be made on them by knowledge rather than by bosses – by objectives rather than by people. They prefer performance-oriented organizations to authority-oriented ones.

A good many knowledge workers tend to tire of their jobs in early middle age – somehow the sparkle, the challenge, the excitement has gone. This problem will not go away, but it can be turned to advantage if it is made possible for the middle-aged knowledge worker to start a second career. The present retirement age of 65 from the first occupation is too late for the majority of knowledge workers – they 'retire' on the job 20 years earlier.

In other fields, notably sport, an individual's career comes to an end much earlier, often in the late twenties or early thirties. In less physical fields of activity, such as commodity broking or investment, individuals in management are frequently described as 'burnt-out' at the age of 35. There is a clear need for career planning and development of a radically different kind from that which is traditional in respect of industrial workers at whatever level.

Some organizations (notably universities) offer periods of sabbatical leave or opportunities for exchange with other, similar institutions as a means of 'recharging' the talented worker's batteries. These practices will certainly become more common in industry.

Maximizing the productivity of knowledge and talent

As was noted in Chapter 4, knowledge can be transferred from A to B without diminishing the amount that B has. Drucker (1969), for example, has drawn attention to the key role of knowledge transfer in the growth of the multinational enterprise since, as an economic resource, knowledge has the distinctive characteristic that when moved from the USA to France it is a net import to France and an increase in France's capital stock, but there is no corresponding decrease in the American stock of knowledge capital.

The same is largely true of talent in other fields. The great violinist does not diminish his talent by coaching young violinists, nor does the professor of English literature's command of his subject become diminished with each tutorial he gives. If anything, the contrary is true. Thus, as many organizations have clearly recognized, the key to maximizing the productivity of talent is to multiply it and the most effective way to multiply it is by training.

Once again, IBM can be quoted as a model of the progressive corporation. In *The IBM Way*, Rogers (1986) describes the practice, approach and philosophy behind IBM's training programmes. IBM sales and systems engineer trainees get one year's initial training – nine months in the field at a branch and three months in one of IBM's National Education Centres. A training manager at the branch will supervise a trainee's programme which will include self-paced learning modules ranging from the company's culture and values to basic product knowledge. Trainees accompany experienced staff making company calls. They make their first product demonstration before a critical group of experienced representatives. At the Education Centre learning to sell begins on the second day of the course. The syllabus covers the company's support structure and how to use it, an analysis of the competition and an introduction to business skills.

Whereas many companies give the task of training new people to their least productive or 'burned-out' sales staff, IBM believes that the sales force is far too important for its training to be left to mediocre people. It employs its top sales staff as instructors for periods of 18 to 24 months and gives them training in teaching methods. The instructor/trainee ratio is 1 to 10 and in addition top marketing and systems engineering staff act as guest lecturers.

A key method by means of which much of the sales training is given is the 'Armstrong Case' – a fictitious international company which is highly diversified with a hotel chain, retail stores and manufacturing subsidiaries. The case material includes detailed profiles of Armstrong's key executives, covering personality characteristics, attitudes and past decisions. Instructors play the roles of personnel and trainees are required to call on them and face a range of challenging situations. The exercise culminates in a simulated customer meeting and a presentation of the 'IBM solution'. IBM also involves real customers in the training process which greatly heightens the sense of reality.

IBM believes that a weak sales training programme leads to high turnover of sales personnel – which costs more than an effective training programme. In recent years IBM lost less than three per cent of its first-year marketing representatives.

Despite the strong evidence from companies such as IBM and Marks and Spencer that training pays off, a surprising number of companies still pay only lip service to it. In other fields of activity than industry most western countries fall well behind the standards of training and coaching provided by some Soviet-bloc countries for athletes or those in the performing arts. Gary Kasparov, world chess champion, describing his way of life in Britain's *Sunday Times* in 1986 told how he spends much of his time in a training camp at Baku on the Caspian sea. Chess players of international standard live there in the best possible environment, not only studying chess and preparing for games, but training physically to improve fitness.

In a democratic society, an organization can own land, capital and equipment, but it cannot own the human resource. This is an important difference underlying the way in which we must manage in the information era. A knowledge worker, if mismanaged, can always walk out of the door and find another challenging job, perhaps with one of our competitors. That is why it is so important to understand the soul of the organization and to accommodate to the deepest values and needs of the knowledge workers who are the ultimate strategic resource of an intellectual organization.

William F. Miller
Managing Intellectual Organizations
SRI International 1986

'Knowledge' or 'Talent' accounting

A system of 'knowledge' or 'talent' accounting would make it possible to arrive at an approximate measure of the extent to which the organization is 'knowledge' or 'talent' intensive and from that point on to measure any changes in either direction. Even more important it would provide the basis for a performance measurement of a new kind (beyond the productivity of labour or return on capital employed) – the return achieved on the talent or knowledge employed in the business.

A simple first approach would be to break down all costs under headings as follows:

A *Knowledge or talent costs*
- Employment costs of all kinds above the level which currently applies to unskilled labour (including recruiting costs, pension funding, allocation of over-

head of personnel function).
- Cost of all education and training.
- Cost of all bought-in knowledge* or talent – accounting, auditing, legal, management consultancy, equipment servicing and repair, etc.
- Cost of all books, reports, journal subscriptions, memberships of professional associations, costs of attendance at conferences.
- Licence fees, royalty payments.

B *Other costs*
- Capital costs: depreciation on plant and equipment; interest and dividends; cost of materials, work in progress and stocks.
- Energy costs: employment costs up to basic labourer's rates; costs of non-human energy – electricity, gas, coal, etc.
- Miscellaneous costs: rates; services such as water, telephones, etc.

The ratio of A to B will indicate the extent to which an organization is knowledge- or talent-intensive. Similarly, the ratio of A to total sales revenue will indicate the rate of return on knowledge or talent employed.

Such an approach, is, however, clearly too simplistic. As has been pointed out, it overlooks the fact that much of the knowledge or skill purchased by a firm is contained not in the minds of people, or in books, discs, tapes or other conventional stores of information; it is built into plant and machinery. In this sense, therefore, an organization can become more knowledge-intensive by purchasing advanced technology as well as by recruiting graduates. This needs further analysis and explanation.

Every good that is made and every service that is supplied is

---

* A complicating factor which needs analysis in order to refine this approach further is that some knowledge is clearly imported in the form of plant and machinery. It is difficult, however, to gauge the 'knowledge content' of a piece of equipment as an element in its cost. For example, a word processor brings with it more knowledge than a typewriter, but what element in the cost difference reflects this? Much of industry's capital expenditure in fact involves buying knowledge which is encoded in metal rather than on disc or tape. The traditional way of looking at capital as a factor in production has its origins in a time when the only significant form of capital was land and overlooks this altogether. This point will be returned to later.

produced by combining, in differing proportions, three elements:

1   Human knowledge, skill or talent.
2   Energy – whether supplied by human beings, animals or, via machines, by fossil fuels or atomic fusion.
3   Material resources – land, minerals that come out of the land, things that grow on the land.

This is true both of final or consumption goods and of intermediate, or production goods.

What people are prepared to pay for final goods depends partly on their perception of how *much* of each of these elements there is, in the final product, and on the *quality* of each. It also, of course, depends on what they desire the object for. If, for example, a painting is bought as an object of aesthetic joy, the only thing that matters is the skill or quality of the artist. If it is by Picasso or Matisse, that determines its value and no attention is paid to how much energy was expended in making it – either by the artist or by those who made the frame and canvas. Indeed, to be told that the artist 'dashed it off' in a matter of minutes is likely to cause admiration rather than its opposite. Nor does anyone bother to estimate the likely cost of the materials – canvas, wood and paint. On the other hand, if the picture is being bought as a piece of furniture – to fill a space on a wall or compliment a colour scheme – then relatively more attention will be paid to such questions as the cost of the materials used in making it.

In the same way, business organizations, when purchasing intermediate goods, will be influenced in terms of the price they are prepared to pay by the relative amounts of knowledge, materials and energy included in the product. In extreme cases the source of value is clear. In the case of a management consultant's report, clearly it is the value of the 'knowledge' element which determines the price, not the value of the paper it is printed on. (Even so the consultant will aim to impress upon his client the value of the report by using high-quality paper, good bindings and making sure that the report is sufficiently 'weighty', literally as well as metaphorically.) A somewhat different example is the numerically-controlled machine tool. Here the source of value is much less obvious, since considerable amounts of energy have been used in making it and it contains a considerable amount of high-quality steel. It is still being bought, however, for the built-in knowledge that comes with it and which the purchaser believes will give competitive advantage. Without that built-in knowledge the machine has merely scrap value. For purposes of knowledge accounting, therefore, one possible procedure would be to take the cost of the machine less its scrap value into the accounts as a knowledge input. Other intermediate goods, which have little or no knowledge content, would then be accounted for as largely or wholly physically inputs.

At the risk of making the argument too complex to be useful or practical, two further points need to be made. First, a distinction needs to be made between the knowledge that has been used in making the product and the knowledge that has been built into the product for the purchaser to make use of. The 'knowledge value' of a word processor lies in what it will do for the user, and not in the vastly greater field of knowledge which was drawn upon when it was being made. Also, it is important to distinguish between knowledge or talent which is already commonly available which will have one value and one price, and knowledge or talent which is innovative and which will provide the user with a sharp competitive edge, thus justifying a much higher value and price.

Difficult as these conceptual distinctions are, it is likely to be even more difficult to apply them consistently in practice, particularly in ways which will satisfy not only shareholders and auditors committed to traditional accountancy practice but also Inspectors of Inland Revenue. Given, however, that it is possible to agree sums of money to stand for such intangible assets as goodwill it ought not to be completely impossible to place a value on the knowledge content of a new piece of equipment.

A complementary approach is to make sharp differentiation between different types of capital expenditure, each of which has a different purpose.

1 Capital expenditure specifically aimed at achieving competitive advantage (i.e. relative to the competition, reducing costs, improving quality or enabling innovation of new products) by means of importing into the company

new knowledge, developed by other organizations, but available only on the basis of its being built into plant and equipment. Examples would include computers, word processors, numerically-controlled machine tools, computerized typesetting systems, etc.

2 Capital expenditure aimed merely at replacing *existing* plant and machinery and thus not bringing any increment to the purchasing company's stock of knowledge. (This is equivalent to renewing a licence to continue to use some increasingly obsolescent knowledge.)

3 Capital expenditure on buildings and vehicles.

On this somewhat simpler and more practical basis, expenditure under the first heading would be accounted for as a 'knowledge input' while expenditure under the second two headings would not.

It should be stressed however, that these are preliminary issues for others, far better qualified so to do, to work upon and develop. The alarming thing is that nearly 20 years after Drucker's appeal for 'knowledge accounting' so little has been done to develop the subject.

Summary

Management of knowledge- or talent-intensive organizations is a largely uncharted field. It includes two issues, however, which are of great importance and which have been addressed by various management writers. First, there is the question of managing or motivating knowledge workers or talented personnel. Secondly, there is the difficult issue of accounting for knowledge and its outputs in the same way that traditionally the outputs of capital and labour have been accounted for. Each of these has been discussed in this chapter, but it should be emphasized that the intention is merely to open up the subjects and expose them both to wider debate and more detailed analysis.

10　Managing cultural change

The basic philosophy, spirit and drive of an organization have more to do with its relative achievement than do technology or economic resources, organizational structure, innovation and timing.

Thomas Watson

In 1970 Alvin Toffler, invited by the giant US corporation A T & T to study and report on its future strategy, decided to try to identify some of the basic beliefs which had helped make the company so successful over the years (Toffler, 1985). He discovered that many of them had been formulated by Theodore Vail who had led A T & T at the turn of the century. Vail was a 'radical manager' rather than an 'incremental manager', that is to say he believed the business environment of the time was undergoing a profound transformation which demanded some fundamental changes in the business in response. Vail understood the nature of the changes taking place in industrial society during his time and in the light of that understanding was able to shape A T & T into an organization perfectly adapted to its time and place.

Toffler listed some of Vail's beliefs:

- Men are chiefly motivated by economic reward.
- The bigger a company becomes, the stronger and more profitable it is.
- Labour, raw materials and capital, rather than land, are the primary factors of production.
- The mass production of standardized goods and services is more efficient than handcraft production.

- The bureaucracy, in which each sub-unit has a permanent, clearly-defined role in a hierarchy, is the most efficient form of organization.
- Technological advance brings progress.
- Work, for most people, must be routine, standardized and repetitive.

Throughout the company's early years, standardization was the dominant theme. For the first half of the 20th century the company's motto was 'one policy, one system, universal service'. It led to a single, starkly simple corporate goal – saturation of the market – putting a standard black telephone into every American home. This was a gigantic undertaking. As late as 1940 fewer than 40 per cent of US homes had telephones installed.

In its day, this simple concept of standardization was revolutionary. Its adoption in the automobile industry, by Henry Ford in particular – any colour you like 'as long as it is black' – is frequently cited as the principal feature of the 20th century's mass production phase of industrialism. This standardization was applied not only to the product, but to operating procedures, manufacturing techniques, personnel and training matters – indeed every aspect of the corporation's functioning.

A T & T had risen to be one of the world's largest and most successful corporations in an age of mass markets, mass production, uniformity and conformity. In the 1960s, however, as Toffler clearly saw, a new diversity of life-style, taste and preference was growing strongly. He raised the issue of what this new diversity meant for A T & T, dedicated as it had been to standardization. It might well respond superficially to market forces by introducing new models, a range of colours and styles, or new services, but could it respond at a deeper level – could it accept and implement the organizational changes which would be necessitated by market segmentation? Could it, in effect, change its *culture*?

As the market demanded more and more variety the company was faced with shorter and more varied production runs. As the range of services offered increased, the company had to invent new routines for dealing with them. But as the number of manufacturing or service 'standard routines' grew, the frequency with which each was used fell. People were having to learn to cope with enormous variety, their work became far less routine and repetitive. What Toffler describes as a 'choking sense of complexity' came to pervade the company. To deal with it called for far more sophisticated management, new kinds of people and a willingness on everyone's part to abandon those cherished beliefs about the values of routinization, standardization and bureaucratic organization which had historically underpinned the company's success – in short, a cultural revolution.

My Fifty Years with Ford

It isn't the incompetents who destroy an organization. The incompetent never gets in a position to destroy it – it is those who have achieved something and want to rest on their achievements who are forever clogging things up.

Charles Sorenson (1959)

What *is* corporate culture – and does it matter?

All organizations have a culture – a set of beliefs, widely shared, about how people should behave at work and a set of values about what tasks and goals are important. Deal and Kennedy (1982) distinguish between values to do with objectives or goals, such as excellence, service, quality or progress, and 'instrumental' values which are to do with *how* such goals are to be achieved – for example, IBM's emphasis on respect for the individual. Values are sometimes expressed in short pithy phrases, for example:

- Universal service (A T & T)
- The world's favourite airline (British Airways)
- Productivity through people (Dana Corporation)

Such slogans are not necessarily part of a strong corporate culture. In Britain, for example, Marks & Spencer's strong culture is not summed up in a simple phrase. At the same time many company slogans are simply advertising messages and bear little or no relation to the underlying culture of the firm.

Deal and Kennedy (1982) argue that the solution to America's industrial malaise (and by implication, that of Western Europe also) cannot be found by adopting Japanese management methods or by applying the analytical tools and models of the business schools, but by relearning old lessons about how culture ties people together and gives purpose and meaning.

There have been several attempts by social scientists to develop classifications of types of organizational culture. In the 1960s, in the UK, Burns and Stalker (1962) identified two distinct types of culture in the electronics industry – the organic and the mechanistic. The organic culture was characterized by informality, little emphasis on hierarchy and status, lack of clarity in respect of structure and job specifications, strong emphasis on overall corporate objectives and considerable lateral communication. The mechanistic culture, by contrast, involved strong emphasis on functional specialization, precise definition of duties, powers and responsibilities, communication vertically via the chain of command, and reliance on formal written orders and instructions. The organic culture appeared most effective in rapidly changing environmental conditions, while the mechanistic culture was more suited to conditions of stable routine.

This simple two-fold classification was further developed by Sadler and Barry (1970) in studies of firms in the printing and construction industries. They took as a starting point the idea that Burns and Stalker's observations reflected variations along two quite distinct variables – control and integration. Control refers to the extent to which people's behaviour is prescribed by higher authority on the one hand or left to the discretion of the individual on the other. Integration refers to the extent to which the activities of the organization are closely co-ordinated in relation to achievement of the overall task.

Taking these two variables into consideration results in the four-fold classification of types of culture shown in Figure 10.1. The *integrated bureaucracy* is a culture which involves considerable emphasis on control, authority, rules and procedures but which also emphasizes co-ordination of effort in the direction of achieving the organization's overall task or goals. The *mechanistic* culture also emphasizes control and authority but has a strong emphasis on functional specialization

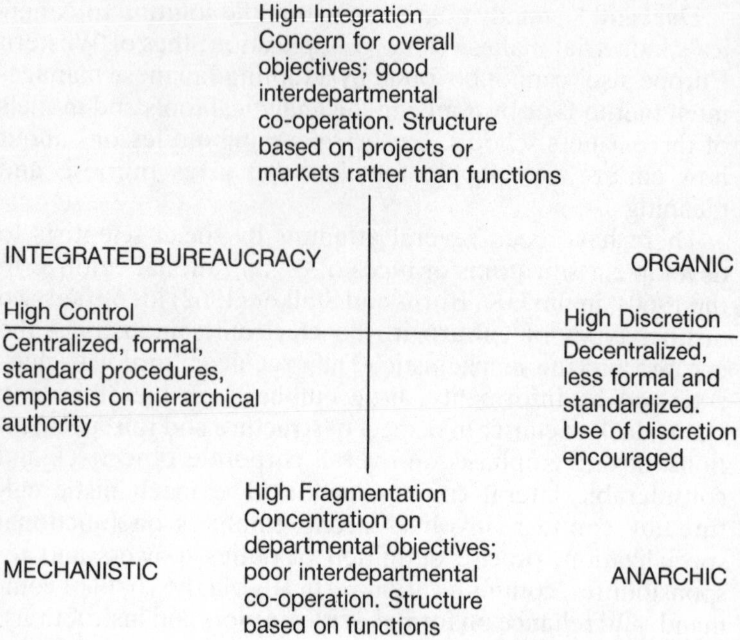

High Integration
Concern for overall
objectives; good
interdepartmental
co-operation. Structure
based on projects or
markets rather than functions

INTEGRATED BUREAUCRACY   ORGANIC

High Control   High Discretion
Centralized, formal,   Decentralized,
standard procedures,   less formal and
emphasis on hierarchical   standardized.
authority   Use of discretion
                                                      encouraged

                    High Fragmentation
                    Concentration on
                    departmental objectives;
MECHANISTIC   poor interdepartmental   ANARCHIC
                    co-operation. Structure
                    based on functions

Figure 10.1   Four main types of organizational culture

with the result that there is relatively low concern with overall
objectives. The *organic* culture emphasizes both individual
discretion and autonomy, on the one hand, and teamwork
in the interests of achieving overall goals, on the other.
Such a culture involves a great deal of mutual trust – senior
managers must trust those lower down to use their discretion
in the interests of the company as a whole and those at the
lower levels must trust their seniors to support them, particularly when the decisions they take involve risks. Finally, the
anarchic culture is one characterized by low control and low
integration. Such a culture can be appropriate in situations
where the activities involved are highly creative or indi-
vidualistic and can be carried on independently of each other.

A similar typology of cultures is offered by Charles Handy
(1985). His four culture 'types' are:

- The *role* culture   This is virtually identical with the
                        integrated bureaucracy.
- The *task* culture   This is similar to the organic. It is

above all a team culture where the objective of the team's work is a common factor uniting people.

- The *person* culture
This is very similar to the anarchic culture – the individual is the central point and so far as there is a structure or system it exists only to serve the individuals within it. Such cultures are typically found in barristers' chambers, architectural partnerships and other professional firms.

- The *power* culture
Rather like a spider's web the power culture is dominated by the individual at the centre – an entrepreneur or highly powerful chief executive; as a result it is a highly political culture and one in which decisions are taken on the basis of who possesses power rather than on purely logical or rational grounds.

A very similar classification has been offered more recently by Harrison (1987) who uses the terms *role* culture, *achievement* culture, *support* culture and *power* culture to describe four social systems virtually identical to those described by Handy.

Another type of business culture, one that does not feature in Handy's or Harrison's list, but which certainly must be included, is the family firm. Although this does have some characteristics in common with the power culture, the second or third generation family business (which may by today have grown to international or global proportions, and which may well be subject to extremely wide share ownership) is nonetheless, a very distinctive type of culture and merits separate consideration.

In such cultures, families have founded dynasties. They still exercise huge influence if not actual power or control. Various myths and traditions about the family exist, and the family atmosphere of paternalism remains. The 'family' in such cases is usually an expanded one to include not only in-laws, but also members of other families closely connected to the original or founding families over several generations.

In such cultures there are only basically two groups of people – the 'family' and all the others. (It is however possible to pass from one group to the other, either by marriage or by becoming so accepted by the family as to be invited to join the inner circle.) Although family firms can embrace the most modern technologies and can in many ways be extremely sophisticated, they characteristically retain a number of archaic practices, particularly in the personnel field. Family firms tend in turn to employ whole families, and several generations of workers serve in the same organization, thus adding to the sense of family which abounds. When faced with key decisions family firms suffer from two distinct problems. First, each and every decision will be looked at in terms of whether the outcome is likely to strengthen or weaken family control of the business. Secondly, each and every decision will be looked at not only in terms of how it affects the business, but what impact it will have on relationships within the family.

Like entrepreneurial cultures, family firms face problems of succession. Also, like entrepreneurial cultures, their ability to adapt depends on the speed of response of those at the top and the appropriateness of adaptation depends whether the family can be persuaded to move the business in the right direction at the right time.

The amount of agreement between these and other studies of corporate culture indicates that distinct types of corporate culture do, indeed, exist, although in practice particular organizations may well combine elements of more than one of these cultural types.

The three principal forms appear to be power culture, role culture or bureaucracy, and task or organic culture.

Power culture

This culture can vary according to the source of the power, the objectives of those who exercise the power, and their ability, judgement and competence.

The power may be held by an individual – either the entrepreneur who has founded the organization, or, at a later stage in the organization's development, by a strong, charismatic or authoritarian chief executive. Alternatively, power may be wielded by a group of people – usually a family.

Organizations with power cultures can achieve outstanding

levels of performance in cases where the person or group holding power has a strong sense of direction, is capable of exercising sound judgement and making the right decisions, and by one means or another can build up loyalty and commitment throughout the organization. Where all or any of these attributes is lacking, or in cases where those holding power are not particularly concerned to achieve an outstanding level of performance, the results can range from the mediocre to the disastrous.

A weakness of power cultures is their tendency to lose their most able people if those people feel that, however able, they will not be able to have a full share in the decision process. The loyal team of lieutenants which remains may be made up of mediocre 'yes men'.

Another Achilles' heel of even the most successful power cultures is, of course, the succession problem. A prime objective of current holders of power in highly successful companies of this type must be to plan for a smooth transition of power and to build a culture capable of continuing to achieve standards of excellence following the demise or departure of its original inspiration.

Role culture, or bureaucracy

This culture is commonly found in public sector organizations as well as in business. There appear to be two main types – the integrated or 'ideal' bureaucracy in which the rules, procedures and structure which govern behaviour ensure both tight control and close co-ordination of activities, and the mechanistic, functional, or fragmented bureaucracy, in which different parts of the organization fail to co-ordinate their activities (at best) or are in conflict (at worst).

Bureaucracies work well under certain conditions – a stable environment within which a highly routine or standardized task is being carried out by a workforce which is not, on the whole, highly educated (with the exception of an élite class of top-level administrators) and which, above all, is not expected to be creative, innovative, questioning and challenging the accepted ways of doing things. Industrial bureaucracies were ideally suited to the era of mass production and represented the classical ideal in terms of organization structure for the early management theorists such as Taylor, Fayol and Urwick. The values of the bureaucratic spirit – rationality, order, integrity, service, impartiality, efficiency, standardization, conformity, seniority and the like – served to unite people in a common concern for 'doing things right'. The Achilles' heel of the bureaucracy, however, is that doing things right becomes more important than doing the right things.

In the course of very many studies of large industrial bureaucracies over a period of twenty years the Research Department at Ashridge Management College has identified a number of cultural factors in common among poor performing organizations (some of which have gone out of business or have been taken over during the period). These are:

1   Complacency, bordering upon arrogance, accompanied by a deep scepticism about the value of corporate strategy, the need to study the competition, and the need to invest in education and training (particularly management training).
2   Conservatism – lack of receptiveness to new ideas, resistance to change, hostility to new technology.
3   Production orientation, accompanied by strong scepticism about the value of marketing.
4   Functionalism – concern for functional boundaries and professional rather than organization standards of performance.
5   Status and seniority are greatly emphasized. High-ranking officials are held in awe. Issues such as company cars and executive dining rooms are extremely important.
6   A secretive, closed climate in respect of information. A very high proportion of documents and communications are classified as 'confidential'.
7   Tolerance of incompetence, low output norms and poor-quality service pervades the organization. Excuses for failure are always forthcoming and are acceptable. In particular, it is rare that decisive action is taken to deal with very senior management who have ceased to perform effectively or who have developed behaviour problems such as alcoholism.
8   Scepticism about the importance of human motivation, commitment, involvement in decision-making and leadership in promoting organizational effectiveness.

9   Divisive personnel policies, treating white-collar and
     blue-collar employees as quite distinct classes of people
     both in respect of terms and conditions of employment
     and working conditions. In particular the culture treats
     blue-collar workers in a largely instrumental way, re-
     cruiting them and laying them off again as business
     fluctuates.
10   A tendency to treat rules and procedures as ends in
     themselves, rather than as means to an end, coupled with
     strict adherence to the boundaries of jobs as laid down in
     job descriptions: 'That's not my responsibility'.
11   A masculine culture in which only lip service is paid to
     equality of opportunity for women and in which women
     will rarely be found occupying key line management
     jobs.
12   Insularity. A tendency to treat the organization as if it
     exists for the benefit of its members; hostility towards
     customers who are often quite literally seen as the
     enemy; ignorance of and little or no curiosity about
     broad trends in the business environment.

This portrait of a 'sick' industrial bureaucracy or public
agency may sound extreme – sadly, it isn't. The principal
challenge facing organizational leadership is to take cultures
of this kind and to transform them into the kinds of culture
described below.

Task, or organic culture
This type can also take a variety of forms. What they have in
common is that power is widely distributed, and that it is
associated with expertise, competence, talent and performance rather than with financial control, office-holding,
seniority or even personal charisma. (The paradox about this
type of culture is that it is frequently created by a person or
group wielding great power but deciding to share it and
redistribute it in the interests of organizational effectiveness.)
Another frequent starting point for this type of culture is a
professional partnership of architects or accountants.

The values of the task or organic culture include achievement, innovation, competence, teamwork, trust, openness,
personal growth and development, autonomy, creativity, and
risk. It is a culture suited to a rapidly-changing environment

and to a highly-educated and articulate workforce. It is essential as the setting for much work in the service industries where the frontline worker must exercise discretion and judgement on behalf of the organization in situations where he or she cannot refer either to a supervisor or to a rule book.

These cultures can emphasize teamwork or individual performance according to the nature of the task. It is vital, however, that the goals of the organization as a whole should not be lost sight of. Once teams start working independently or individuals are allowed too much discretion to pursue their own hobby-horses the organic culture can rapidly degenerate into anarchy.

The main common features of organizational culture of this kind include:

1   Concern for the individual. This involves investing in his or her training and development, providing as much job security as possible, and not discriminating between classes of people (blue-collar versus white-collar, men versus women).

2   Building teams. Project groups, temporary task groups crossing disciplinary boundaries are given greater emphasis than traditional formal hierarchic structures.

3   Concern for achievement. Goals are clearly stated. High performance standards are set and achieved. Above-average performance is publicly and appropriately recognized. Promotion reflects achievement rather than seniority. Poor performers are dealt with humanely but not left in key positions.

4   Belief in productivity through people. Considerable emphasis is given to leadership, motivation, job satisfaction, etc.

5   Outward looking – to the customer and the market generally, but also to the competition and the business environment generally.

6   Openness and trust. Information is widely shared and sensitive issues openly discussed.

7   Delegation, decentralization and discretion. Authority is pushed down the organization as far as possible and employees encouraged to use their own judgement and discretion.

8   Innovative. New ideas are welcomed – indeed they are actively sought.

Some firms are already beyond rescue; they are organizational dinosaurs. These are non-adaptive corporations, many of which will disappear between now and the not too distant turn of the century. Companies with household names and famous products; companies with assets in the billions; companies with tens, even hundreds of thousands of employees; companies with enviable reputations on Wall Street and seemingly unassailable positions in their markets – all are at risk.

Alvin Toffler (1985)

This list has much in common with the characteristics of winning companies identified by Peters and Waterman (1982) in the USA and Goldsmith and Clutterbuck (1984) in the UK. There is a growing international consensus that for the western countries economic renaissance is dependent upon the cultural transformation of large-scale business, and in particular on the extent to which decaying bureaucracies can be replaced with dynamic organic cultures. Alvin Toffler's view (1985) is that for many famous companies it may already be too late. However, this may be too pessimistic. Some very considerable success stories of cultural change already exist and as managers increasingly come to accept the need to achieve cultural change and acquire the skills to bring it about more will surely follow.

Changing corporate culture

Rosabeth Moss Kanter (1983) sees cultural change in organizations as involving five main forces:

1   *Departures from tradition.* Activities occur, usually at the 'grass-roots' level, that deviate from the organization's traditions or norms. Either new people tackle old problems in new ways or new problems arise calling for fresh approaches. When successful, new patterns of behaviour are capable of more widespread adoption – they become 'solutions looking for problems'. A high proportion of such departures from the traditional result from the ac-

tions of 'entrepreneurs' who are striving to move beyond the constraints imposed by existing rules and procedures.

2   *Crisis or 'galvanizing event'.* Changes of a major nature which demand a response. These can be environmental (for example, the oil crisis), or a severe business recession, or internal (for example, adoption of a new technology).

3   *Strategic decisions.* Strong leaders emerge to indicate a clear path to the future, building on existing capacities and strengths and exploiting both the previous successful experiments in departing from tradition and the sense of urgency created by the crisis.

4   *Individual 'prime movers'.* People who can turn the vision into reality by persistence, commitment, powers of communication, example.

5   *Action vehicles.* Changes take root when they become embodied in multiple concrete manifestations. Training programmes, travelling roadshows, videos, publications, reward and recognition schemes, steering committees.

Big organizations, as a rule, only change significantly when certain pre-conditions are met. First, there must be enormous external pressures. Second, there must be people inside who are strongly dissatisfied with the existing order. And third, there must be a coherent alternative embodied in a plan, a model or a vision.

Alvin Toffler (1985)

Other writers give the greatest emphasis to the role of leadership and to the importance of the leader's vision of the organization's future. Warren Bennis and Burt Nanus (1985), for example, argue that in order to provide an organization with a sense of direction a leader must develop a 'vision' – a mental image of an achievable and desirable future state of the organization. It can be 'as vague as a dream' or as precise as a quantitative expression of objectives.

When an organization is given a clear sense of its purpose and direction the individuals who belong to it are able to identify themselves both with their roles in the organization and with the organization's role in society. This has a powerful impact on their motivation to achieve. It generates enthusiasm, energy, pride, effort – a culture which can be felt very quickly when dealing with the organization. Bennis and Nanus (1985) quote Polaroid and Sears and Roebuck as examples. It also makes it possible to distribute decision-making widely – people know what to do without having to appeal to higher levels in the organization because they know what end results are to be looked for. The basic distinction between leadership and management, they argue, is that the leader works with the emotional and spiritual resources of the organization whereas the manager is more concerned with the physical resources.

An outstanding example of the achievement of cultural change through brilliant leadership in the military sphere is the story of the Burma campaign in the Second World War. In 1943 General Slim took command of a defeated British army in Burma. Characteristics of the culture he inherited included despondency, lack of confidence in leadership, and belief in the invincibility of the Japanese enemy – all reinforced by a record of defeat and a feeling of being a 'forgotten army'. Slim (1956) saw the need to concentrate his energies on building morale – to create an organizational culture characterized by commitment, self belief, confidence in leadership and pride in achievement. He thought deeply about the nature of morale and concluded that it needed spiritual, intellectual and material foundations.

The spiritual foundation exists when men believe in the organization's objectives and feel that what they do contributes to the achievement of them. The intellectual foundation exists when men believe the objectives *can* be attained and have confidence that they belong to an efficient organization with competent leadership. The material foundation exists when people feel they are getting a fair deal, that they are supplied with the equipment and tools needed to do the job and that working conditions are as good as they can be.

In common with other great leaders Slim stated the objective in the simplest terms: 'to destroy the Japanese army – to smash it as an evil thing'. He then communicated his vision of 'defeat into victory' personally, to all ranks, behaving in his own words 'more like a parliamentary candidate than a general'. He spoke to every combatant unit, usually standing on the bonnet of his jeep with the men gathered around. He often made three or four such speeches a day. Always he gave them the same message and with the same purpose. He told them what the objective was and how it was going to be achieved. It worked.

Some of the specific leadership acts performed by Slim are worth noting. First, he articulated a simple, clear goal – to destroy the Japanese army. Secondly, he communicated this *personally* to the rank and file. Thirdly, he showed it could be done by achieving some early successes on a small scale. Fourthly, he started a newspaper to record these successes and to spread the news widely and rapidly. Fifthly, he built loyalty and commitment in various ways. For example, when he took up the appointment he did not follow common practice of bringing his own staff officers with him – he took over the existing staff, thus placing his trust in them and demonstrating his confidence in their abilities. Also, he insisted on equality of treatment of all who served under him – British troops, African units and Indian formations were all to be treated alike and he strictly forbade the development of élite or 'crack' units.

Finally, he demonstrated (often dramatically) that he would not tolerate incompetence or slackness in his subordinate commanders. Malaria was causing more casualties than the enemy and he instigated a strong drive to reduce its incidence. He ordered spot medical checks on units to find out what proportion of the troops had been taking their mepacrine tablets. If the overall result in a unit was less than 95 per cent he sacked the commanding officer. After he had sacked three the message got through and the incidence of malaria cases fell dramatically.

In more general terms, the task facing the leader in achieving cultural change involves several stages:

- The desired culture must be specified in terms of goals, values, beliefs, appropriate behaviour and ways of embodying these abstractions in more concrete aspects of organizational life.
- The existing culture must be analysed so as to assess what changes need to be made in order to align it with the desired culture.
- The necessary changes must be implemented.
- The results must be evaluated.

● Measures to reinforce and maintain the new culture must be taken.

The leader must not be blind to the difficulty of the task facing him if he is to achieve fundamental and lasting change. The whole process might take between five and fifteen years depending on the size of the organization, the length of its history and the strength of its traditions. The more successful the organization was in the past, the more difficult it will be to change it. (So many companies have great and glorious pasts stretching ahead of them.)

It is also vital to transcend the superficial, verbal level and achieve real behavioural change. The values that people espouse or profess often bear little relation to the ones which really guide their behaviour. As a result, probing corporate culture calls for very sophisticated and time-consuming techniques, usually involving highly-qualified diagnostic consultants using such methods as unstructured depth interviews, employee attitude surveys and content analysis of company literature and documentation.

Edwin Baker (1980) lists ten techniques which leaders of organizations can use to influence corporate culture:

● *Role modelling.* The manager sets the example by behaving in ways consistent with the norms and values the organization wishes to reinforce. (For example, the chief executive of a Disneyland theme park picks up any litter he sees as he moves around.)
● *Face-to-face communication.* As in the case of General Slim, taking time to visit employees on site and address them personally. (Using a video is a very dangerous alternative and can have disastrous results.)
● *Written communication.* Company newsletters, posters, books (for example, Thomas Watson's *A Business and its Beliefs* – the IBM bible).
● *Positive reinforcement.* For example, if you say you believe in developing people, then reward and give recognition to those who do so.
● *Recruitment policy.* Those people who fit the desired culture or who will be capable allies in achieving cultural change.
● *Promotion and transfer decisions.* Ensure that people

- who embody the desired culture are moved into key positions.
- *Training*. Ensure that all training, especially induction training covers company philosophy and is as concerned with attitudes and values as with methods and techniques.
- *Personnel policies*. Such as single status, abolition of time clocks, no lay-offs.
- *Physical factors*. Cleanliness, good housekeeping, use of colour, quality of employee facilities, open-plan offices, no executive car parking facilities, quality of customer reception facilities.
- *Showmanship and symbolism*. 'Roadshows', conventions, slogans, badges, supporting advertising campaigns.

Summary

1 All organizations have a culture – a set of beliefs, widely shared, about how people should behave at work and a set of values which order goals and tasks in terms of their importance.
2 The answer to the industrial malaise of the West will be found in changes in corporate culture – the basic philosophy, spirit and drive of an organization – rather than in new management techniques and methods.
3 The West's great and *consistently* successful corporations such as IBM, Proctor and Gamble, General Electric, Marks & Spencer and Mars became great because they developed strong cultures.
4 From the many studies of corporate culture three main types emerge:

- Power culture
- Role culture or bureaucracy
- Task, or organic culture

5 The culture most appropriate to the closing years of the 20th century is the task or organic culture. With the marked exception of the entrepreneurial start-up venture, organizations based on the exercise of power are becoming less acceptable, particularly in the eyes of young, highly-educated, achievement-oriented employees. Bureaucracies simply cannot cope with rapidly changing

conditions and do not provide challenging and satisfying jobs or career structures for today's young managers.

6 Corporate cultures *can* be changed, although some kind of crisis which *demands* a response will probably be needed before a profound and lasting change can occur.

7 In bringing about cultural change, the role of leadership is paramount. The leader must have a vision of the culture to be achieved and the skill, energy, determination and persistence to bring it about.

Appendix

The possibility of bringing about significant improvement in business performance by means of changing the culture of an enterprise is regarded with some scepticism by many senior managers. That it is, indeed, possible is best demonstrated by practical examples which show not only what has been achieved, but how it has been done. This appendix describes the process in several highly-successful cases.

British Airways

In 1983, Colin Marshall, newly-appointed chief executive of British Airways, defined the focus of the state airline's business as service and the corporate goal as giving the best service. He understood very well that service excellence depends on knowing what the market wants together with the ability to respond quickly to customers' changing needs and expectations. He also knew the importance of being adequately resourced and having an appropriate organization structure. Above all, however, he recognized that service is given by people and that excellence in service requires a corporate culture in which a caring and committed management is as concerned about the needs and expectations of the employees as it is about those of the customers.

Marshall's highly-successful attempt to change British Airways' culture involved several interrelated strategies:

- The issuing of a statement of corporate mission to express the objectives and values of the organization.
- The introduction of a management training programme entitled 'Managing People First' (MPF).
- Introducing a performance appraisal system (known as MENTOR) designed to appraise just those aspects of management performance (particularly leadership of staff) focused on by the MPF programme.
- A performance-related reward system designed to reinforce the desired behaviour.
- A project (known as the Seeds project) designed to select and train senior line managers not only to act as trainers on the MPF programme but generally to serve as models of the kind of management behaviour required and to

take part in other organizational development projects.
- Customer service training (known as Putting People First) for all staff having direct contact with customers.
- The development of a training programme for new managers (The Young Professionals) to ensure the adoption of a consistent management style.
- The setting up of a task force, the Human Resources Strategy Board, under the chairmanship of the chief executive, to plan change and monitor its results.

The objective of the Managing People First programme was stated as 'to substantially enhance the participant's personal performance as a manager of others'. The qualities to be developed were a sense of urgency, vision, motivation, trust and willingness to take responsibility. The learning process was divided into three parts:

- Identification of each participant's specific strengths and weaknesses by means of confidential feedback given by outside consultants based upon questionnaires completed by the participant, his or her associates and subordinates.
- Practice in developing the skills needed to remedy weaknesses and improve management performance.
- Preparation by the participants of a detailed plan for the improvement of his/her performance back on the job.

Marshall's statement of the values underlying the new approach are summed up in a series of statements which together constitute the 'BA Way'. the key elements are:

- Identification with corporate mission and goals
- A sense of urgency and energy which enthuses others
- High personal standards
- Demonstration of personal and emotional commitment to the British Airways mission
- Belief in own and organization's ability to succeed
- Willingness to take calculated risks and responsibility for success or failure
- Having a 'can do', positive attitude
- Willingness to take the initiative
- Having creative and innovative ideas which are also capable of practical application
- Being sensitive to the impact of change on others.

By the autumn of 1985 British Airways was able to announce to its staff that they had been named airline of the year for the second year running by the magazine *Executive Travel*. They also placed British Airways top in six of the ten separate categories for which it was eligible, including most preferred transatlantic carrier, most preferred carrier to the Middle East, premier carrier to the Caribbean, Central and South America, and best UK domestic carrier. Cabin crew took top positions in best overall cabin staff and most helpful cabin staff sections. The airline's food and wine was voted best and the British Airways business class service was also voted top.

In the same year UK travel agents voted British Airways top in the two main airline categories, best in Europe and best transatlantic.

Essochem Europe – developing the long term view
Essochem Europe covers the Middle East and Africa as well as Europe and in 1986 had sales of 2.5 bn dollars. The company has eight product lines, five of which could be described as commodities and three as speciality chemicals.

Manufacturing takes place at eleven different European locations and the company is organized as a matrix combining product lines and geographic areas. David R. Clair, who took over as company president in 1981, has given an account (Clair, 1986) of how he articulated a vision of the company's future and brought about a radical transformation of culture.

Clair took control of the company during the most prolonged recession in the history of petrochemicals. He spent his first two years reducing manpower, cutting costs and controlling capital expenditure. During this difficult period, however, he did not ignore longer term issues and in 1982 a middle management development programme on the theme Managing for High Performance was begun. Participants in this programme indicated that they were uncertain about the company's longer term goals and in consequence felt frustrated in their attempts to apply the lessons of the training in practice. A further cause of frustration was the fact that their seniors had not been exposed to the same ideas. As a result, a similar programme was developed for the company's vice presidents and chief executives of subsidiaries. At this point, Clair prepared a first draft of his vision of where the company should be heading in the long term. This included correcting the company's basic weakness – its heavy dependence on commodity chemicals with the associated vulnerability to economic downturns. More imaginatively, his vision foresaw the company becoming a first class chemical organization by demonstrating success in both commodity and in speciality markets.

The draft of the vision statement was included in the papers given to the participants in the new programme for top management. It generated a great deal of interest and the ensuing debate led to a final version which was then widely communicated within the company. The vision was briefly and simply expressed under three headings – the visions, the goals and the path.

The visions	● Become a first class chemical company
	● Be successful in both commodity and in speciality markets
The goals	● Be the lowest cost producer of commodity chemicals
	● Significantly increase the percentage of speciality products in the mix
The path	● Continued emphasis on process and product technology
	● Superior cost control systems for each commodity product
	● A broad based emphasis on new product development and marketing
	● Fully exploit cross-product line opportunities
	● People empowerment – gain commitment of total workforce
	● Success. The customer is our best barometer.

The strong people empowerment theme in the vision was regarded as critically important for its success. It was also vital that the commitment of the top management team should be highly visible, with a high level of face to face interaction between the president and staff at all levels. Various task forces were established to facilitate change, including a change committee consisting of four senior managers responsible for assessing where the organization currently stood in relation to the ideal as described in the long term vision. A great deal of work was put into refining and developing systems and procedures; for example, the appraisal system for supervisors and the system for cost control.

Perhaps the most challenging task was to develop the product mix so as to achieve higher added value. This involved an approach called 'incremental everywhere' – a broad-based attack on the problem including within its scope all product lines, functions and subsidiaries.

In his account of the change process, Clair describes how the meaning of leadership became much clearer to him. The elements he felt essential included listening, thinking through in broad terms where an organization should be going and how it could get there, communicating that direction effectively, assessing the organization's cultural strengths and weaknesses and its potential for change. It also involves starting and maintaining many different initiatives and being a 'consistent and visible missionary' who is clearly committed to change, both intellectually and emotionally. Most important of all it means empowering the workforce, helping people to give of their best. Clair also points out, rightly, that in the field of cultural change in organizations there is no such thing as a quick fix. It requires patience, persistence and the expenditure of huge amounts of energy so as to prevail over the forces of indifference and inertia.

ICI – a company of the twenty-first century now

The role of transformational leadership in bringing about cultural change in a large organization is well exemplified by the case of ICI, Britain's largest chemical concern.

ICI's home market represents only one twentieth of world demand for chemical products, yet it has the widest sales network of any company in this industry. It is the world's fifth largest chemical company, but of all the leading international businesses in chemicals it is the one with the best stock market record in recent years.

When John Harvey-Jones was appointed chairman in 1982 the company had reported two successive loss-making quarters. He was, on the surface, an unlikely choice for the job. He joined the company at the age of 33 from the Royal Navy in which he had served since his schooldays, and moved steadily up the ICI promotion ladder. He made progress despite knowing no chemistry and despite his colourful, unorthodox persona, characterized by long hair and large, colourful ties, which he explains as a reaction against about 20 years of naval discipline.

He took an early decision to adopt a high profile and become a very visible chairman. In consequence, his beliefs about organizations and how they change have been well articulated in numerous interviews, articles about him in the media, and finally in a book he has written since retirement (Harvey-Jones, 1988).

These beliefs can be summed up as follows:

1 *A determination to be the best* – in this case to create the best chemical company in the world.
2 *Patience*. The knowledge that such an objective can only be achieved by solidly and carefully building a new company culture.
3 *Breadth of vision*. His idea of 'best' did not just embrace profitability. His vision of the best company included being the best in bringing in new products; in market sensitivity; presence; range; quality; how the company dealt with people; ethical, environmental and safety standards.
4 *Taking the long term view*. Seeing his success or failure as judged by where the company would be five years' later.
5 *A leader, rather than a manager*. Leading by example and persuasion, and by hard work, not on the basis of power or authority. Being able to help others release their energies and focus their efforts on corporate objectives; creating conditions in which people want to give of their best.
6 *Humility*. Detesting 'red carpet' treatment, subservience, hierarchy and flattery. Being willing to own up to making mistakes.
7 *Openness*. Trying to make ICI a more open and friendly organization and one in which constructive criticism of top management is accepted.
8 *Compassion*. During his years of office ICI shed 60,000 jobs – something he genuinely feels sad about.

During John Harvey-Jones' period of office the tangible results of his style of leadership speak for themselves. Turnover rose from £7.4bn. in 1982 to £10.1bn. in 1986 while profit before tax rose more dramatically from £259m to £1,049m. In 1984 ICI became the first British company to announce pre-tax profits of £1bn.

Harvey-Jones' main specific actions during his period of office were:

- *Radical change in the product mix.* At the start of the 1980s almost two-thirds of ICI's profits came from bulk chemicals. This proportion fell to one-third by 1987, while the profits from high added-value speciality products correspondingly grew. For example, there was considerable growth in the field of pharmaceuticals. ICI's Inderal is now the world's third best selling drug.
- *Change in market mix.* Dependence on the UK market has fallen from 37 per cent of sales to 25 per cent, while sales in the US now account for 22 per cent of the total compared with 15 per cent at the beginning of the decade.
- *Strategic acquisitions.* Since 1980 ICI has acquired over 100 companies. The most notable were Beatrice Corporation (US) with its product range of speciality films, lubricants and finishes and Gliddon (US) which resulted in ICI becoming the world's largest paint manufacturer.
- *Rationalization and reorganization.* Thirty thousand jobs were cut in the UK without causing serious industrial relations problems. The group's bulk chemicals activities were brought together in a new subsidiary, the Chemicals and Polymers Group, combining petrochemicals, fibres and agricultural products, employing 38,000 people with sales of £4bn or 40 per cent of total turnover. This consolidation is expected to bring huge cost savings as well as improved research and development payoffs. Head office functions were drastically pruned, decision-making substantially decentralized and the number of executive directors reduced from 12 to nine.

These achievements are notable for the speed with which they were brought about. Making such major changes in large organizations in the time scale involved can only be done if there is a massive shift in culture. ICI began to accept the need for this after disastrous results in 1980 when, after extraordinary items, the company showed a net loss of £20m and its share price fell by 54 per cent. John Harvey-Jones was chosen as the man to lead such a transformation and he proved equal to the task.

ICL – A 'lame duck' revitalized

Simon Caulkin, writing in *Management Today* (Caulkin, 1987), described the transformation at ICL as a 'Lazarus act', in which the strategy, shape, organization – the whole organizational culture – were radically altered in one of the most sweeping sets of changes in the recent history of British industry.

ICL has not, over the years, performed in a consistent or convincing fashion. Twice rescued by the government and regarded as a 'lame duck', it was taken over in 1985 by STC. This was seen as a rescue operation, yet since then ICL has outperformed its new parent.

The company's previous culture has been described as product oriented, functionally structured, rule-bound, and combining bureaucracy with a degree of flair. The process of changing this was started in 1981 by a new top management team, Robb Wilmott and Christopher Laidlaw. They adopted a market-led strategy based on two concepts. First, the company would become an information technology company, offering services and solving customers' problems, rather than making computers. Secondly, it would focus its limited resource on clearly defined market segments. A number of industry related business centres were set up, the first of which concentrated on retailing, and supermarkets in particular.

ICL has since built up market leadership in this field in the UK and has won substantial orders overseas. In the USA it has achieved success with a specialized software package tailored for chains of large do-it-yourself and home improvement stores.

The company also strengthened the range of technology available to it by means of collaboration agreements with other companies – most notably with Fujitsu.

Wilmott's strategic vision was followed through and translated into durable cultural change by Peter Bonfield. Although British, Bonfield, like Wilmott, came to ICL from the US electronics company Texas Instruments. Bonfield brought about a radical restructuring of management, creating a complete matrix system based on business centres aimed at public administration, defence, manufacturing and financial services as well as retailing. Caulkin describes the process of organizational change as 'agonizing', pointing out that it was much more than just redrawing the organization chart. To get a product dominated, highly centralized compartmentalized company to restructure itself around marketing specialisms involved a cultural transformation. The chief means employed to bring this cultural revolution about was a very substantial management education programme, the main achievements of which have been described by Christopher Lorenz (Lorenz, 1986). He listed the following as fundamental improvements resulting from the training programme.

● Acceptance of the hard fact that ICL was a small company seeking a means of surviving in an IBM world.
● The consequent recognition that there was no choice but to focus on narrow market segments where ICL could establish and maintain market leadership.
● Realization that a competitive edge can result from superior marketing or organization as well as technological leadership.
● Willingness to swallow corporate pride and buy Japanese technology.
● The creation of a new breed of general manager.
● The creation of a common conceptual framework and a common language for communication about strategy, marketing and organization.
● The ability to respond quickly to change.

Organizational renewal: the Jacobs Suchard experience
Klaus Jacobs, Chairman and Chief Executive, has described the process of cultural change following the merger of Jacobs and Interfood (Jacobs, 1987).

At Jacobs Suchard, the last few years have been marked by a very deliberate special renewal effort linked to two needs.

● The need to create an entirely new Jacobs Suchard organization and management philosophy following the 1982 merger between Jacobs and Interfood, each with widely differing management cultures.
● The need to shape a uniquely entrepreneurial, unbureaucratic, fast-moving, cost-effective organization to

continue building Jacobs Suchard's worldwide market position in the face of increasing competition.

Historically, Jacobs was a German coffee company. Jacobs' expansion became blocked in coffee markets and therefore looked to diversification for further growth. This led in 1982 to a merger with Interfood, itself the product of a merger between two leading Swiss confectionery companies, Suchard and Tobler.

At this point a major organizational renewal effort was launched, focused simultaneously on the challenges of the Interfood integration and on shaping a new corporate posture to cope with an increasingly competitive environment.

In this renewal effort, Jacobs Suchard found these elements to be most important:

● Setting expectations and standards of excellence.
● Setting certain corporate themes or rallying points around which to build the organization: in this case, the product names 'Jacobs' and 'Suchard', the notion of the 'hybrid consumer', the importance of trade marketing, and being an 'enterprise of entrepreneurs'.
● Reducing the number of levels in the organization and eliminating middle management bureaucracies.
● Empowering people.
● Selectively invoking temporary 'martial law' to deal swiftly with priority issues that would normally be the responsibility of decentralized business units.

Expectations and standards

In a series of 'direction setting' meetings, top management discussed with operational managements what it was that was expected of them. The aim was to be not just as good as the competition, but better.

Everyone needs a flag to march under, a special theme or themes that set their organization apart from others. These themes must be simple enough for everyone to understand, and directly relevant to their business. Jacobs Suchard chose six themes around which to build the new organization.

1 Location. Since the merger of Jacobs and Interfood had taken place in Switzerland they were both Swiss companies in the European environment.

2   The product names 'Jacobs' (for coffee) and 'Suchard' (for confectionery). The name Interfood meant very little to consumers, trade customers or employees.
3   The hybrid consumer. From consumer research it was discovered that many of their customers were becoming much more discriminating in their purchases. The same customers, for example, would buy premium products in one category and private label products in another. This phenomenon became known as 'the hybrid consumer'. Serving the hybrid consumer became a major force behind product development and marketing efforts.
4   Integrated trade marketing. In Europe, grocery manufacturers and retailers have historically been on difficult terms. In this competition for value added both were losers, since the resulting lack of cooperation added costs at the interface between them. Jacobs Suchard decided to launch an effort to expose these system inefficiencies and commit the company to a programme of promoting efficiency through more open trade terms.
5   An 'enterprise of entrepreneurs'. Jacobs Suchard resolved to concentrate the best management talent in the country-based business units, ruthlessly stripping away as many as possible of the intervening management layers between them and top management in Zurich.
6   Excellent employees and employers. The changes within the organization all require care not only to have the best talent on hand to fill top positions, but to breed and educate young talent.

Unlayering the organization

As already mentioned, the company made a determined effort to eliminate as many as possible of the intermediate layers, through a variety of experiments ranging from outright elimination of a whole organizational layer to assigning 'godfathers' as coaches and counsellors without hierarchical authority or responsibility.

Key people resource

A fourth process was to attempt to obtain more value from key people resources, particularly at headquarters. First, the direction-setting meetings were used to get top managers out in to the field, participating up-front in setting business priorities. Second, they were encouraged to allocate their personal time selectively among the various country organizations, concentrating their hands-on time with those in greatest need of help. Finally, in some cases some key headquarters managers were made responsible for certain country organizations, in addition to their ongoing responsibilities.

Temporary martial law

A fifth step was to deliberately invoke temporary 'martial law' in order to deal centrally with some important production and marketing issues. For example, some chocolate products, such as Toblerone, were being produced in as many different shapes and formulations as there were manufacturing countries. Some countries were producing certain products in sub-economic quantities, while modern facilities were lying underutilized in neighbouring countries.

Role of corporate center

Klaus Jacobs' philosophy of management can be summarized as follows. The biggest barrier to renewal is organizational stability. It is critical that there be relatively frequent changes at the top. Such changes (1) encourage managers to focus on the overview rather than just on their own particular responsibilities, (2) foster teamwork, (3) help prevent creeping bureaucracy. There is no more important responsibility of a chief executive than to ensure perpetuation of the enterprise. It is a task that entails constant renewal efforts.

It is very much the responsibility of a company's top management to ensure that key people are motivated and rewarded. Working in a highly competitive field requires an immense amount of sustained effort. To generate this effort requires (1) the challenge and ultimate satisfaction of excellence, (2) more than generous psychic and monetary rewards, and (3) the realization that working hard for success is entirely compatible with one's family and other personal interests – and with having fun as well.

11 Developing managerial leaders

If it is accepted that western society is undergoing rapid and radical transformation it follows that the institutions and organizations which survive and prosper will be those most capable of adapting to a changed world.

This process of adaptation is unlikely to occur in the absence of powerfully effective leadership of the kind which Tichy and Devanna (1986) refer to as 'transformational leadership'. We need men and women of vision, creative and innovative people, capable of getting others to share their dreams and to work with them to reshape and redirect the strategies and tactics of organizations.

The bureaucratic systems of administration which grew up in a more stable era and which were based on the evident need to standardize and routinize patterns of behaviour in large, complex organizations, are particularly vulnerable in times of rapid change. Bureaucrats must be replaced by leaders if organizations are to adapt.

It is also true that in times of change people feel a need for leadership. The feelings of uncertainty and insecurity which accompany rapid change cause people to seek reassurance and a sense of direction from those who know where they are going and can inspire confidence and trust.

In the absence of the traditional sources of motivation to work (the sheer need to survive, reinforced by a strong work ethic in society) organizations need leaders capable of generating enthusiasm for goals such as quality or productivity. When power doesn't work any more leadership comes into its own.

Finally, organizations need innovators, not just people with new ideas but people able to carry new ideas through into action – into new products or new processes – persuading others to support the changes and disruptions that inevitably accompany significant innovation.

The nature of leadership

Acts of leadership can be observed going on around us in daily life – at work, in the home, in the community. Each act of leadership involves two stages: first, a person knows what he or she wants to happen; secondly, he or she successfully influences or persuades others to help make it happen. It is the same process, whether it involves one child saying to his or her friends 'Let's play hide and seek' (and they do) or a supervisor at work saying to the members of his or her section 'Let's stay on tonight until we've finished this job' (and again, they do). What the leader wants to happen may be as trivial as a game of hopscotch or as grand as a vision of an economy with zero inflation or full employment. The common thread is that the leader actually wants change. He or she is not content with the status quo or, if discontented, is not willing to sit around waiting for someone else to produce the ideas for changing it. It is of little value to have ideas for change, however, if you cannot persuade others to support you. Leaders are people who can get others to comply without exercising force or authority. When this involves massive change to the established order we can speak about *transformational* leadership.

From this analysis can be spelt out what is involved in being a leader:

- A need or desire to 'take charge' to make things happen, to seek change.
- The ability to see clearly in which direction to go.
- The ability to convince others – including, possibly, people you cannot interact with face to face – to support you.

Leadership and management

Do organizations' leaders also need to be managers? In the context of complex organizations the answer must be a firm 'yes'. It is not enough to have new ideas or to be able to inspire others to follow. The goals of leadership must be congruent with the goals of the enterprise and the means adopted to achieve them must be the most economic compatible with achieving the aim. This is another way of saying that *effective* leaders in organizations must be able to exercise managerial functions such as planning, budgeting, scheduling work and monitoring performance against targets. They must be able to function effectively within the inevitable constraints imposed by organization structure and by the operating conditions derived from the organization's environment. They must, in a word, be *managerial* leaders.

Training for managerial leadership

Being an effective managerial leader is more difficult than being a competent administrator. This has always been so, but is particularly true of managerial leadership exercised in the context of modern industrial and commercial life. Today, leaders in most organizations stand naked and exposed before their followers, revealed, like the Wizard of Oz, to be ordinary people. The protective layers of power, authority, status, remoteness, ceremony and decoration have been steadily stripped away. The four-star general, looking at himself in the mirror before leaving for the parade ground, is reassured by the smart uniform, the 'scrambled egg' on his cap, the gold braid of his badges of rank, his medal ribbons. His appearance in front of his troops involves ceremonial drama as the officers and men spring to attention and the salute is given. There is no doubt who is in charge. Much the same applies to other traditional leader roles which pre-date the modern industrial enterprise, for example the priest in his robes, the policeman or hospital matron in uniform, the town mayor with his resplendent chain of office.

One of the greatest failings in most organizations is that there is no one to tell the emperor that he has no clothes.

Tichy and Devanna (1986)

By contrast, the managing directors of today's business organizations look in their mirror as they leave for the office and see just another smartly dressed figure approaching middle age with greying hair. They will soon stand, indistinguishable from others, on the station platform. On reaching the office they will squeeze into a crowded lift along with the rest – many of whom probably have no idea who they are. For them to be able to reach out to the members of the organization, inspire them with their vision, persuade them to make sacrifices to work with them to achieve it, is an enormous challenge. That challenge is repeated at every level of the organization and the closer to the shop floor the less likely is it that any props such as status symbols or remoteness can be called upon to help.

When young men and women enter officer cadet school in the armed forces they are carefully selected for their leadership qualities. They are then given intensive training in leadership skills. This training continues, albeit less intensively, when they have become commissioned officers, and culminates in training for strategic leadership when they reach very senior ranks. Managers in industry are more likely to be chosen for their functional or professional expertise than for their leadership qualities; they have in many ways a more difficult leadership task than service officers; yet in the great majority of cases they receive no training at all for leadership.

Until recently, leadership has not featured prominently in the education and training of managers. Certainly the word leadership is rarely encountered in the descriptions of the content of MBA programmes in North America and Europe and published lists of the short courses available for experienced managers include very few which are concerned with the subject. There are several factors which have contributed to this neglect. There is undoubtedly an association between leadership and the military and a related tendency to associate training for leadership with physical 'outward bound' types of activity. Another is a genuine doubt as to whether qualities and skills of leadership can be learned in the same way, for example, that accountancy or economics can. At a deeper level, however, lies a belief in the power of rationally-designed systems to generate organizational effectiveness. It is this belief that has caused management trainers and management consultants to place so much emphasis on control systems, information systems and planning systems and such systematic ways of regulating human behaviour as work study, management by objectives and performance appraisal.

If it is accepted that training for leadership is vitally important, and that leadership performance can be improved by training, then appropriate and effective learning methods must be developed.

Clearly there is likely to be very little that can be learned about leadership from sitting in classrooms listening to lectures on the subject, although there will almost certainly be some value to be derived from interaction with successful leaders. Even here, however, the benefit is much more likely to be gained as a consequence of challenging, questioning and response rather than from politely listening to tales of old campaigns.

As far as 'off the job' leadership development is concerned, learning is achieved in three principal ways which are frequently combined in a single exercise:

- Practising leadership
- Observing the success/failure of others acting in a group task of some kind
- Receiving feedback from instructors and/or peers while participating in some group process

Practice in leadership normally takes one of two forms: indoor exercises such as leading a group discussion, running a meeting, or acting as leader in a more complex group task such as building a construction of some kind or planning an operation such as famine relief; and outdoor exercises, leading a group during an experience which normally combines some degree of physical danger (rock climbing, canoeing, abseiling, etc.) and some degree of physical deprivation (getting cold and wet, going without hot food, etc.). These exercises are designed to simulate real-life situations, in that they involve problem solving, stress, the need to inspire teamwork, conflict resolution, the maintenance of morale, and the exercise of interpersonal skills.

Both indoor and outdoor approaches are subject to criticism – the indoor exercises are 'unrealistic' in the sense that it doesn't really matter whether or not the problems contained in the exercise setting are satisfactorily resolved. The problems lack, therefore, both realism and a sense of urgency. In consequence they fail to generate stress in the same way that real-life situations do. By contrast, the outdoor situations are 'for real'. Bad decisions can lead to groups losing their way, experiencing acute discomfort, even real danger. Risks to life and limb are carefully controlled but are present to a sufficient degree to generate stress. The weaknesses in this approach are, however, obvious. The situations involved in abseiling, canoeing and orienteering are radically different from those involved in mergers, technological change and global competition. The stress generated is much less in the case of the more athletic members of the group, especially those who are experienced and skilled in the types of outdoor activities involved. The 'outward bound' type of activity is clearly more appropriate for younger managers than for those already in senior posts.

There appear to be two alternative approaches. One, which appears not to have been attempted to any great extent, is to expose managers to real-life situations which are stressful in other ways than exposure to physical dangers and discomforts and which can therefore be assumed to be close parallels for organizational leadership. Examples of tasks of this kind might be:

● Plan and provide a day's outing for mentally-handicapped children.
● Plan and execute a presentation to senior pupils in a comprehensive school to persuade them of the desirability of a career in industry.
● Plan and conduct a survey of attitudes of young people in ethnic minorities towards job opportunities and discrimination in employment practices.

The other approach, which has been used particularly in developing chief executives (as described later in this chapter), is to use the leader's own work situation and the problems arising therein as the main vehicle for learning. Nothing can be more real than the job itself. If people are to learn from experience, however, they will need skilled coaching and counselling and the opportunity to receive feedback.

In the same way, observing the success or failure of others in the leadership role and receiving feedback from others about one's own leadership behaviour, are likely to be more effective sources of learning when carried through in the context of reality than when related to artificial situations and groups of people brought together solely for training purposes.

The creative side of leadership

Creative leadership involves the following processes:

- Generating, or stimulating others to generate, original ideas for new products, new ways of doing things, ways of solving problems.
- Evaluating the ideas generated in this way and selecting ones worth pursuing.
- Convincing the rest of the organization that an idea is worth investing time in and worth the trouble of implementation.

What abilities and skills are involved?

First, it is not necessary for creative leaders to have the ability to have original thoughts and ideas – it is much more important that they should be able to recognize, value, and champion the original thoughts and ideas of others. It is, in fact, dangerous when leaders have a rich flow of original ideas since they are unlikely to be very objective when evaluating them. If they use their power to champion their own ideas they run two risks. One is that the idea is not, in fact, a very good one. The other is that although the idea is good it will meet with resistance because members of the organization resent their use of power to push their own ideas rather than other peoples'. (The only exception would be in the case of quite outstanding innovative ability in which case other creative people would be likely to leave the organization.)

Secondly, creative leaders must be able to foster creativity in others. How can they do this? Most people have learned by experience to be cautious with their 'bright ideas' and to hold them back to the point where they have become absorbed into conforming moulds. The cartoon showing a chief executive sitting at a conference with his heads of departments and exclaiming 'I want your frank and honest ideas; don't hold back, even if it costs you your job!' strikes home to all of us. To clear away the inhibitions and release creativity involves doing two things – helping people gain insight into the influence of their past experience on their present behaviour and attitudes and creating the settings or conditions that actually encourage creativity. Any activity, exercise or mental practice which tends to dissolve or disrupt fixed associations will be helpful in giving people insight into the sources of rigidity in their own frames of reference. One example is to engage in brainstorming sessions in which judgement about the quality of ideas is deliberately deferred.

Leaders work in an environment that sees creativity as a threat, especially creativity defined as a deviant response. The deviant response is something that could ruin an organization as easily as it could move it forward. So organizations tend to be designed for survival, not for creativity and managers are embedded in an organization that runs contrary to most of the things that we know about creativity. In fact, most organizations might have a sign that says 'stamp out creativity'. Many organizations deal with creativity by isolating it, controlling it, judging it and, at times, eliminating it.

Morgan W. McCall Jr (1979)

Seven ways to cultivate creativity in organizations

1   *Really* reward good ideas from suggestion schemes.
2   Show how highly you value creativity – sponsor artists, bring their work into the organization.
3   Encourage individuality and self expression rather than conformity and standardization. Don't impose a uniform way of dressing, or standard office furnishings. Offer a wide choice of company cars.
4   De-emphasize hierarchy, status, seniority, etc.

5 Symbolize creativity in choice of corporate image and house style.
6 Make sure people get out and visit other organizations, particularly ones in different cultural settings.
7 Build networks made up of individuals from different backgrounds and different perspectives on life.

The special needs of chief executives

The evident gap between society's need for leaders and supply has highlighted the key role played by those appointed to direct and control organizations. A nation's achievements in many spheres – economic, social, technological and cultural – obviously depend to a large extent on the quality of the performance of people in jobs such as managing director of a business, hospital unit general manager, head teacher of a school, director of an art gallery or head of a research laboratory. Allowing for obvious differences between the public and private sectors, between organizations varying in size and in the nature of the missions to be accomplished, there are some common elements in these jobs, indicating some common training needs. Some indication of the nature of these has been obtained in the course of a series of programmes held at Ashridge since 1980, known as Action Learning for Chief Executives. Participants in these programmes meet in sets (of about five persons) with a set adviser. The sets meet for one day at a time at intervals of about a month for six months or more. An evaluation study of these programmes has recently been carried out by Dr Ian Cunningham (1986).

With few exceptions, the chief executives attending these programmes felt they had benefited greatly, yet there was no attempt to feed them with any functional knowledge nor to teach them any management techniques. Instead they became involved in a subtle and complex process of learning about leadership; the starting point of this process is for each participant in turn to expose to the other members of his or her set a real-life problem or issue confronting him or her in his or her role and to seek their help in resolving it. In the ensuing interaction such problems become redefined – even lost sight of altogether; but in the process chief executives gain insights into their own and others behaviour and attitudes which result in change.

Not all the participants were clearly able to articulate precisely how and why their behaviour had changed as a result of the process. Among the comments which were reasonably explicit the following example probably sums up the feeling of many:

> I keep struggling with the word 'self-realization', which is awful really, but it is probably the nearest I can get. I think it changed me from being put in a job where I didn't know how to do it and being a little bit worried that I not only didn't know how to do it but that the little devils had got their knives out ready to carve us into little bits. I think it helped to get me through a period where I certainly realized that probably nobody ever knew what to do anyway – you make it up as you go along. The fact that you get a title like managing director shouldn't actually mean that all the answers are there.

... all of a sudden it occurred to me that there was more to this whole business and my life than what is going to happen tomorrow or next week. What is important is what has happened in the past and what is going to happen in the future. . . . These things changed my perspective and I started to watch our business differently. . . . Once I got the reins I knew what I was going to do.

Jack Sparks
Chief Executive Officer
Whirlpool Corporation
(quoted by Tichy and Devanna, 1986)

More recent experience in training newly-appointed hospital unit general managers confirms the finding that many, perhaps most, chief executives feel they have been put into a job they don't know how to do, that there are people waiting to trip them up, hoping they will fail, but that having assumed the mantle of the boss they must appear omniscient, decisive and totally in command of the situation.

These action learning sets are remedial not only in the sense that the participants are already in chief executive jobs

– they are also remedial in a deeper sense. Several participants used the term 'group therapy' to describe what went on.
One stated 'it helped me enormously. I owe my sanity to the
set.' The experience has, however, pointed to an important
gap in provision for management development – virtually
nothing is done to prepare people to become chief executives.

This statement may seem extreme and will be challenged
from two directions – those in large companies which have
special management development programmes for 'high
fliers' or 'fast track' managers and those responsible for MBA
programmes in the universities. Both approaches to developing general managers tend to concentrate on one aspect only
of the role requirement, and one that is relatively easy to
meet, namely the acquisition of knowledge of the various
management functions and the ability to integrate such knowledge within a conceptual framework which makes it possible
to see the organization as a total system. Little emphasis is
placed on developing other important qualities and skills
which differentiate the role of chief executive from other top
management roles. These qualities and skills are elusive and
difficult to define. They are not quite the same as the 'qualities of leadership' since the latter form part of the attributes
of effective managers and supervisors at all levels.

A vision translated into reality

In the mid-1960s, Tony Williams, chief executive of the Williams
Lea Group, a small family firm in the printing industry, began to
develop his vision of a future which he saw as both inevitable and
desirable. He recognized the inevitability of technological progress and realized well ahead of most other top managers in his
industry that its traditional processes, particularly hot metal composition and letterpress printing, would give way to computer
typesetting and new processes for storing and transmitting information. At a deeper level he saw how the printing industry as
traditionally conceived would dissolve its boundaries and become
part of a wider information processing and communications industry which would operate on a global scale. He observed market
trends and identified the rapidly growing financial services sector
as the market to aim at, moving out of periodical and general
printing ahead of the competition. His vision was wider still, since

he also saw that the massive technological and cultural changes he contemplated could only be carried through with the co-operation of employees most of whom belonged to the traditionally militant print unions. In consequence he embarked upon a programme of social as well as technological change, creating a social climate characterized by risk taking and innovation balanced by openness and trust.

In (1988) he is chairman and chief executive of a substantial group of companies. The turnover of the Williams Lea Group Ltd in the last financial year was £40 million and the profit before tax was £5.7 million. The largest subsidiary – the original Williams Lea and Company – is operating its second-generation computer-based typesetting system and has typesetting links to financial printers in 80 centres, including New York, other centres in the US, Tokyo, and Australia. It handles massive communications tasks in the financial field such as the public flotation of British Airways. At the same time the group has an employee share option scheme which has led to over 60 per cent of employees becoming shareholders in the company and beneficiaries of its record of profitable growth.

Selznick (1984) has argued the difference between 'institutional' leadership and interpersonal or face-to-face leadership. Being the chief executive of an organization differs greatly from leading a department or a project group which is part of an organization. The main differences include the following:

1   Vision – the ability to be sensitive to environmental change and to perceive some future desired state which an organization must attain if it is to survive and prosper.
2   The ability to instill into more people *than can personally be known* both a sense of purpose and a sense of belonging. The chief executive must persuade people to share his/her vision and to feel involved in bringing it about.
3   The ability to act without instruction or even guidance from superiors or support and advice from a peer group; to have warm personal relationships with colleagues yet be capable of dealing with them impersonally and impartially; to experience and live with the isolation and even loneliness that this involves.
4   The ability to use what is often a very considerable degree

of power in the interests of the organization, with integrity and in such a way that justice is both done and seen to be done.

5   The ability to carry a burden of responsibility which is of a quite different order from that carried by senior functional executives – and to carry it in such a way that it does not appear to constitute a heavy burden.

In respect of the development of vision and the ability to be a pioneer or pathfinder, Professor Harold Leavitt (1983), in his Stockton Lecture at the London Business School, said:

> To which occupations and professions then, shall we send our sons and daughters if they, too, wish to become great pathfinders? We might wish to send them to places that appear distant from the contemporary management scene. We could send them to live among artists and architects, or among philosophers and religionists, or among theoretical physicists; but whatever we do, we should not send them to business schools.

The really difficult area is the process of preparing people to shoulder the responsibility, exercise the power and cope with the isolation involved in being a chief executive. Research carried out by the Centre for Creative Leadership (CCL) (Kaplan, 1986) points to a tendency for people to react to this situation in two ways, both of which have adverse implications for organizational performance.

Some let their success and standing go to their heads, when they run the risk of making arbitrary decisions and becoming increasingly isolated from the rest of the organization. This reaction often reflects a brilliant track record thus far which blinds the individual to his or her limitations. The result is the 'I can do anything' syndrome. The chief executive harbours the illusion that he can resolve any problem or deal with any issue single-handed. When inevitably he/she makes mistakes or meets setbacks he finds it very difficult to admit to them and his integrity begins to crumble. When he finally makes a really big mistake the consequences can be shattering for his self-esteem as well as disastrous for the organization.

At the other extreme are those who find it all too much – the expectations concerning calm and firm leadership in times of crisis, the deference and trappings of high office which they feel they have to live up to, the heightened visibility, the public appearances and the like. Such people become inhibited and unable to fulfil their true potential.

The CCL research also highlights the fact that many chief executives are disturbed by the pressure for consistency that goes with heightened visibility. At the top it is very difficult to be seen to change one's mind, to go into reverse, when one has publicly committed oneself to a policy or course of action.

Another CCL study (Lombardo, 1986) points to the importance of values as guidelines for behaviour in the absence of direction from a superior. There is no one to ask 'Am I doing the right thing?' – 'Right' in this context can mean both right for the organization in that the action or decision will lead to improved organizational performance and right in the moral or ethical sense. We are deluding ourselves if we do not accept that these two 'rights' are frequently in conflict, at least in the short run.

How can people be prepared for these aspects of the chief executive's job? There is clearly no simple answer. Yet some necessary component parts of the process can be readily identified. First, the process should involve interaction and exchange of ideas with others – with other potential chief executives, with chief executives who have lived through the experience and come to terms with it and, not least, with people whose roles in society are likely to make them useful sources of guidance and support, for example leaders in different spheres such as politics, religion and the arts.

Secondly, it must involve experience of real responsibility in circumstances which generate significant stress and which involve making difficult decisions and choices. Experience of this kind can best be gained by means of giving people responsibility for carrying through major projects in situations where they have to encounter vested interests, resistance to change and conflicting priorities. This brings us back to action learning and to the acknowledgement that Professor Reg Revans (Revans, 1971) was right when he argued that managers learn from doing things rather than by sitting in lecture theatres. Revans' theories have not received the acceptance and recognition they merit, despite the considerable evidence as to the effectiveness of this approach. Cunningham (1986), for example, quotes an unpublished Local Government Training Board report which had evaluated

various forms of management training experience by local
authority chief executives. The conclusion was:

> It is apparent that the action learning programme had the
> greatest impact on the participants and, even more signifi-
> cantly, there were permanent changes in behaviour applied
> directly to their work and which are still continuing.

Conclusion

The separate and distinct changes which are taking place in the world's advanced economies are not difficult to identify. The principal ones are as follows:

- The emergence of a global economy.
- Within the global economy a shift in the balance of power from North America to the Pacific Basin.
- The growing dominance of the service sector both as a proportion of gross domestic product and as the principal source of jobs.
- Increasing tendency towards over-capacity and over supply in agriculture, and the manufacturing industries.
- The emergence of knowledge and 'talent' as the only scarce resources.
- The development of new and powerful but inexpensive technologies for processing information.
- Shifts in social values, in particular the decline of the work ethic.
- Shifts in the structure and function of social institutions, especially the family.
- Shifts in social structure – the class structure, the occupational structure and the age structure.
- Changes in lifestyles.

Each of these trends is not, however, a separate thread but part of a complete fabric. That fabric has come to be known variously as the post-industrial society, the cybernetic society, the information society, the post-scarcity society and the service economy. It is still in the process of being woven but once the process is complete, society will have been radically transformed.

It is frightening that so few of today's political or business leaders see this clearly. They are either 'incrementalists', acknowledging the necessity, even the virtues, of change but seeing the future merely as an extension of the past; or they are reactionaries, trying to recreate the past, calling for the reindustrialization of their countries or the restoration of the traditional values.

The main task facing institutions concerned with management development is to produce future business leaders, especially future chief executives, who do understand the true nature of the changes currently underway – people who are 'radicals' rather than incrementalists and who grasp fully the implications of the fact that society is not so much changing as being transformed. This task involves several aspects. First, a clear communication of the vision of a post-industrial society and its economic, social and technological characteristics.

Secondly, the development of particular skills to prepare managers for life in the post-industrial organizations. These include the ability to manage *service* as distinct from *manufacturing* operations, the ability to manage 'knowledge workers' and other talented personnel, the ability to manage cultural change in organizations and the ability to make effective use of information technology so as to achieve competitive advantage. Above all, however, the development of the skills of leadership – the ability to have a vision, communicate it, energize others with enthusiasm to bring it into being.

To meet this challenge calls for radical transformation in the content and methods of programmes of education and training for management. In particular, a better balance needs to be struck between training in the analytical, rational and quantitative skills which occupy by far the greater part of most MBA syllabi and issues such as leadership, creativity and ethics which scarcely feature at present. At the same time, learning to manage must take place outside the classroom as well as within it, in particular through action learning, project work and on-the-job counselling and coaching.

The last word can be left most appropriately with Peter Drucker whose work, *The Age of Discontinuity* (1969), was the origin of the thinking and research that has gone into this book. He has said that management is simple, but not easy. The simple part is knowing what to do. The part that is not easy is getting others to do it. It is time for management education and development to focus on the difficult part of the manager's job.

Bibliography

Albrecht, K. and Zemke, R., *Service America*, Dow Jones-Irwin, Homewood, Ill., 1985.

Baker, Edwin, 'Managing Organizational Culture', *The McKinsey Quarterly*, Autumn 1980.

Bell, Daniel, *The Coming of Post-Industrial Society*, Basic Books, New York, 1973.

Bennis, W. and Nanus, B., *Leaders*, Harper & Row, New York, 1985.

Bronowski, J., *The Ascent of Man*, BBC Books, London, 1973.

Burns, T. and Stalker, G.M., *The Management of Innovation*, Tavistock Publications, London, 1962.

Caulkin, S., 'ICL's Lazarus Act', *Management Today*, January, 1987.

Clair, D.R., 'The Long term view' in Adams, J.D., *Transforming Leadership*, Miles River Press, Alexandria, Virginia, 1986.

Cunningham, Ian, *Developing Chief Executives – An Evaluation*, Ashridge Management College, Berkhamsted, 1986.

Deal, T. and Kennedy, A.A., *Corporate Cultures*, Addison-Wesley, New York, 1982.

Drucker, P., *The Age of Discontinuity*, Heinemann, London, 1969.

Goldsmith, W. and Clutterbuck, D., *The Winning Streak*, Weidenfeld & Nicholson, London, 1984.

Handy, Charles, *Understanding Organisations*, Penguin Books, London, 1985.

Harrison, Roger, *Organization Culture and Quality of Service*, Association for Management Education and Development, London, 1987.

Harvey-Jones, J., *Making it happen*, Collins, London, 1988.

Hawker, Paul, *The Next Economy*, Angus & Robertson, London, 1984.

Heskett, James L., *Managing in the Service Economy*, Harvard Business School Press, Boston, Mass., 1986.

Hughes, Philip, 'Are we Living with a Revolution?', paper to IT '82 Conference, London, 1982.

Jacobs, K., 'Organizational Renewal: The Jacobs Suchard Experience', *The McKinsey Quarterly*, Winter 1987.

Kanter, Rosabeth Moss, *The Change Masters*, Allen & Unwin, London, 1983.

Kaplan, Robert E., *The Warp and Woof of the General Manager's Job*. Center for Creative Leadership, Greensborough, NC, 1986.

Leavitt, H., 'Management and Management Education in the West – What's Right and What's Wrong', *London Business School Journal*, Vol. 8, No. 1, Summer 1983.

Lombardo, Michael M., 'Values in Action', *The Meaning of Executive Vignettes*, Center for Creative Leadership, Greensborough, NC, 1986.

Lorenz, C., 'ICL Corporate Renewal – making it happen', *Financial Times*, May, 1986.

McCall, Morgan W., Jnr, 'Conjecturing about Creative Leaders', in Creativity Week 1, 1978 Proceedings, ed. Stanley S. Gryskiewicz, Center for Creative Leadership, Greensboro, North Carolina.

Norman, Richard, *Service Management*, Wiley, Chichester, 1984.

Peters, T.J. and Waterman, R.H., *In Search of Excellence*, Harper & Row, New York, 1982.

Porter, M. and Miller, V., 'How Information Gives You Competitive Advantage', *Harvard Business Review*, 1985.

Revans, R., *Developing Effective Managers. A New Approach to Business Education*, Longman, London, 1971.

Rockart, J.F. and Scott Morton, M.S., 'Implications of Changes in Information Technology for Corporate Strategy', *Interfaces*, 14:1 Jan/Feb 1984.

Rogers, Buck, *The IBM Way*, Harper & Row, New York, 1986

Sadler, P.J. and Barry, B.A., *Organisation Development*, Longman, London, 1970.

Selznick, P., *Leadership in Administration*, University of California Press, Berkeley, 1984.

Slim, W.J., *Defeat into Victory*, Cassell, London, 1956.

Sorenson, Charles, *40 years with Ford*, Cape, 1959.

Stonier, Tom, *The Wealth of Information*, Methuen, London, 1983.

Thompson McCausland, B. and Biddle, D., *Change, Business Performance and Values*, Gresham Paper on Ethics and Business, Gresham College, London, 1985.

Tichy, N.M. and Devanna, M.A., *The Transformational Leader*, John Wiley, New York, 1986.

Toffler, Alvin, *The Third Wave*, Collins, London, 1980.

Toffler, Alvin, *The Adaptive Corporation*, Gower, 1985.

Turner, Graham, 'Inside Europe's Giant Companies. Cultural Revolution at Philips', *Long Range Planning*, Vol. 19, No. 4, 1986.

Index